The Endless Chain of Nature: Experiment at Hubbard Brook

The Endless Chain of Nature: Experiment at Hubbard Brook

PATRICIA PATTERSON STURGES

Book design by Dorothy E. Jones

Published by The Westminster Press®
Philadelphia, Pennsylvania

Printed in the United States of America

Library of Congress Cataloging in Publication Data

Sturges, Patricia Patterson, 1930–
The endless chain of nature.

Bibliography: p.
Includes index.
Summary: Describes the research conducted on a small "closed" ecosystem in the Hubbard Brook Forest in New Hampshire.
1. Forest ecology—New Hampshire—Hubbard Brook Experimental Forest—Juvenile literature. 2. Hubbard Brook Experimental Forest, N.H.—Juvenile literature. [1. Forest ecology. 2. Hubbard Brook Experimental Forest, N.H. 3. Ecology] I. Title.
QH105.N4S83   574.5'264   76–15962
ISBN 0–664–32597–1

This book is warmly dedicated
to the kind and friendly students
who accepted Sheryl and Karen
into the Hubbard Brook community.

CONTENTS

ACKNOWLEDGMENTS

I gratefully acknowledge the assistance of my husband, Franklin W. Sturges, as photographer and scientific consultant for this book. Dr. Sturges began his avian ecological studies at Hubbard Brook as a co-investigator with Dr. Richard T. Holmes of Dartmouth College with the assistance of National Science Foundation grants. He is presently professor of biology and chairman of the science and mathematics division at Shepherd College, Shepherdstown, West Virginia.

I wish to thank Dr. Gene Likens of Cornell University and Dr. F. Herbert Borman of Yale University for the personal courtesies extended to me and my family while we were living at Pleasant View near Hubbard Brook. To Dr. Likens I am deeply indebted for a personal guided tour of Langmuir Ecology Laboratory at Cornell University and for his willingness to share freely his deep concern for and knowledge of our environment and the Hubbard Brook project.

Broad-leaved trees filter sunlight

1

HUBBARD BROOK EXPERIMENTAL FOREST

A post-office box in a small grocery store in West Thornton, New Hampshire, is the summer mailing address for researchers in the Hubbard Brook Experimental Forest. Sharing the White Mountain National Forest with tourists, vacationers, hikers, and swimmers is a team of scientists. They are trying to solve the riddles of water and forest management by discovering how a Northeastern hardwood forest ecosystem works.

The Hubbard Brook Forest is an outdoor laboratory. It is shaped like a bowl five miles long and three miles wide. Ridges rise to make the uneven sides of the bowl. Mt. Kineo is 3,330 feet, the highest point on the ridge. Valleys 750 feet above sea level make the bowl's bottom. Many small mountain streams drain areas of twenty to four hundred acres and flow into Hubbard Brook, which then joins the Pemigewasset River at West Thornton. By this route the water from 7,600 acres of federal forest land flows toward the Atlantic Ocean.

If you visit this experimental forest, you turn onto the Mirror Lake road that joins U.S. Route 3 just before the post office. You pass the lake and then, leaving the paved road, you wind upward into a typical New England broad-leaved hardwood forest. From a high viewpoint you see leaves melt into a solid green quilt that covers the softly rounded peaks, slopes, and narrow valleys of these old, old White Mountains.

Now the forest air is cool, barely stirring. The morning sunlight filters through the leaves, making you feel a bit like Alice, suddenly and unexpectedly stepping into a green wonderland. Entering a Northeastern hardwood forest in the summer is like taking off a sweater, putting on green-tinted sunglasses, and inserting earplugs all at the same time.

As you drive into the forest, the noise of your car engine sounds out of place and disrupts the peace of this place. When you turn off the engine, a sudden quiet makes you feel removed from the outside world.

Be careful when you get out and lean against a tree. Eastern forests have deceptive trees. Outside, a tree may look whole and strong, but insects and woodpeckers may have opened holes to invading molds and fungus that have rotted the tree to its core. Lean against such a tree and it splinters, leaving a jagged stump and a branchy broom, with you lying on the hobblebush vines at its feet.

You stand on the past. Season after season leaves have fallen and piled up. They decayed and were turned over and under, thoroughly mixed through the passing years by worms, insects, grubs, small mammals, amphibians, mites, and reptiles that burrowed through leaves and soil, eating here and discharging there. These animals made pathways for air and water that further broke down leaves, limbs, and bark. A deeper soil was created.

The soil supported a forest that became a home for Indians. For thousands of years Indians used the White Mountain forests without changing the natural surroundings. Their numbers were few. Nature was able to grow over and around their scars. The land kept its natural communities.

But the forest you see is not the one the Indians used so sparingly. After 1763 and the French and Indian Wars, towns grew and settlers cut forests to make pastures for sheep and cows. They cleared land for crops—corn, potatoes, and oats. A lot of timber was cut for lumber. Hemlocks gave tannin for tanning hides. Trees changed into furniture, houses, and many other wood products as well as firewood.

In less than a hundred years, most of the primeval forests had been cut. One half of New Hampshire was under cultivation.

Use quickly depleted the fertility of the thin soil. The land was not good enough to compete with the naturally richer lands opening on the Western frontiers. Dairy and sheep farms failed.

A sawmill, a tannery, a bottling works, a dance hall, a boys camp, and tourist cabins appeared on Mirror Lake's shores at one time or another in its history. So Mirror Lake had periods of pollution. But use was not so great that the little lake wasn't able to clean itself. It has managed to stay a high-quality forest lake with clear water, little decaying plant life, and low nutrient levels. The question is, Will it stay clear under today's high use?

This forest is as important to people today as it was to the Indians and pioneers of yesterday.

The life of a forest and of a human community depend on water. Knowing this, the United States Forest Service has long been the keeper of our watersheds and our forests. States, as well as our national Government,

Road to the outdoor laboratory

have saved much of our country's forests for the welfare and benefit of all the people.

A forest watershed is like a reservoir that holds rainwater when it comes and lets water pass gradually to streams and rivers which serve communities along their flow to the ocean. Because trees are cut for lumber and other products, the U.S. Forest Service wants to know the best way to harvest a forest and control the water that enters streams. What happens to the water-holding ability of the forest when trees are cut in different ways? What happens to the amount and purity (quantity and quality) of water that flows through cutover forests? Trees lose about 40 percent of the water they receive. If the trees are cut, what happens to this water that would otherwise be going into the air through transpiration? Would more water flow in the streams?

To answer these questions and predict more accurately the amount and quality of water reaching downstream cities, towns, and farming communities, the United States Forest Service decided to experiment. They hoped to learn the best ways to manage a forest for the many uses that people demand of it—recreation, drinking water, irrigation water, manufacturing water, timber products, soil conservation, and so forth.

The Forest Service wanted to learn several things. Where did the water come from? How did it move about? Where did the water go and where was it stored? What water was left after all the water-needy parts of the forest had gotten their share? How much sunlight—solar radiation—came into the forest soils? What were the uses of the forest plant cover and what did it give back to the atmosphere?

In their outdoor laboratory the Forest Service hoped to find their answers. They chose this spot because Hubbard Brook's drainage is typical of New England's watersheds. And the boundaries of the watershed bowl kept the water in Hubbard Brook streams. An impervious igneous rock layer—a rock layer with no cracks or holes for seepage—lay below a porous or spongy soil. Water could escape only by evaporation or in the streams.

This combination made a perfect spot for experimenting. All the minerals dissolved in water that came into the forest, or added by weathering or leaching, and all the minerals that went out of the forest could be measured, along with the quantity of water. Water went through the porous soil easily and flowed down the uncracked rock. Heavy rains quickly showed up in the streams that drained the Hubbard Brook basin. Researchers could watch rising floodwaters turn their quiet fishing stream into a roaring lion.

Dr. Robert Pierce was responsible for all the research in the forest. As director of the research projects, he realized the importance of learning everything there was to know about the forest laboratory. He wanted to know the changes in the woods from hour to hour, day to day, month to month, year to year.

He knew that a lot of research would be needed to get the most benefit from the forest experiments that were planned. He was open to new ideas and ways to solve problems. His yes to two ecology professors began the first total ecosystem study ever tried—a "prototype."

The Hubbard Brook ecosystem study was a first on two counts. Such a total study of an entire ecosystem had not been done anywhere else. And cooperation between the Government and private institutions and individuals on a single ecosystem study was also a first in the United States.

The study began slowly. Gradually informal science teams, individual researchers, and Government foresters and scientists worked together to better understand the functioning of an ecosystem. Here scientists from many disciplines could study the links in the endless chain of nature.

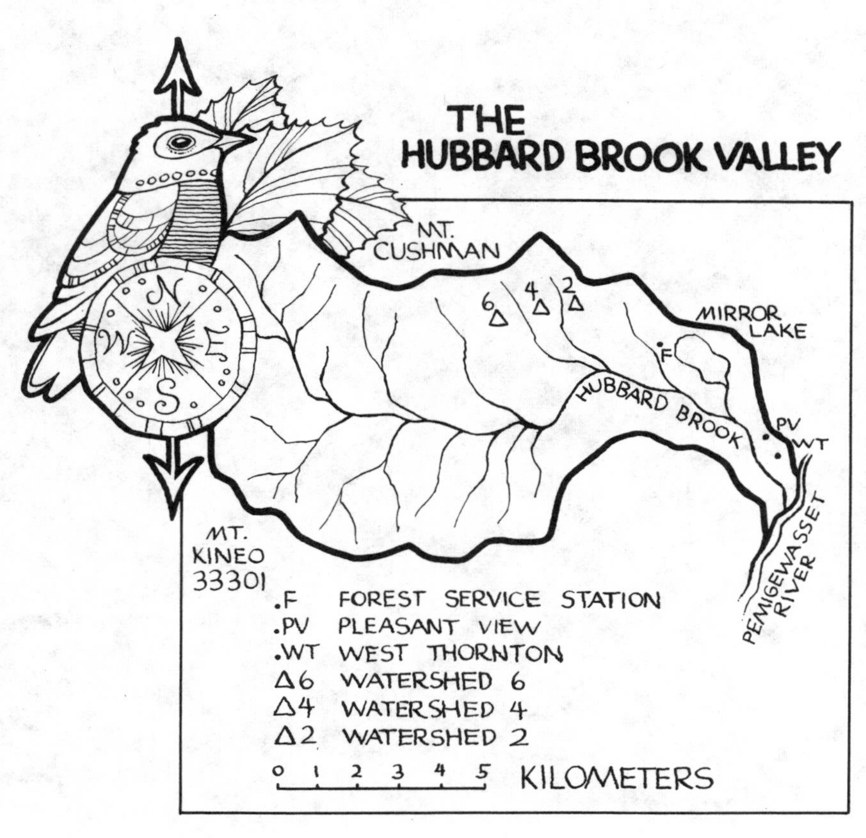

Profile of forest revealed after a cut

2

TWO ECOLOGISTS LOOK AT A FOREST ECOSYSTEM

For its experiment the U.S. Forest Service cut some of the forest. The logs and brush were left to decay. Other strips of forest were also cut but the logs were removed. Some forest strips were left undisturbed to serve as experimental "controls."

Dr. Robert Pierce, manager of the forest experiments, had talked to Dr. Herbert Borman, a forest ecologist, and Dr. Gene Likens, a limnologist. They needed a small watershed to study nutrient cycling. Dr. Pierce agreed to let the two ecologists make use of the forest cutting experiments for their own specialized studies. And so, in 1963, began a cooperative research effort by the United States Forest Service and professors from a private university.

The two ecologists were excited about this outdoor laboratory. Hubbard Brook Forest seemed made for ecologists to study. They could measure everything entering from the air and leaving this forest by way of the streams. They could analyze and compare the experimental strips with the untouched forest. How would the changes made to the strips of forest affect the plants, animals, soil, and water in those same strips?

To you and me the Northeastern hardwood forest seems filled with red maples, sugar maples, birch, alder, beech, and ash trees that tower over our heads, and hobblebush branches that grab at our ankles while we walk on the spongy, often moss-slippery, leaf-covered forest floor. The forest is a quiet, cool, green room protecting us from raucous city noises and the hot summer sun. The plants pour into our lungs oxygen free from sooty city contaminants and smells. The fragrance in the air is fresh and natural. No aerosol woodsy scent is needed here. The forest becomes a place to be alone, to meditate, to observe the animals, to discover flowers and berries, to hike and share a camping experience with friends. What are the things you like to do alone or with friends in the forest? Some of those things may be what ecologists do. But ecologists do many things no one else would think to do.

Dr. Borman and Dr. Likens saw the forest watershed as several ecosystems. Each drainage basin with its own small stream was an individual ecosystem, a small part, a piece, of the whole earth's biosphere or "life" sphere—that part of the earth's land, water, and atmosphere where life can exist. Ecologists look for interrelationships—happenings between the living parts and between the living and nonliving parts in an ecosystem. They look for cause and effect—interrelationships that cause change or balance in an ecosystem.

Let's take the word "ecosystem" apart. "Eco" comes from the Greek word meaning "home." A "system" means many parts working together to make a bigger whole. "Ecosystem" is the way things work together to make a home for the plants and animals, the organisms that live together.

You yourself are an example of a system. Your lungs, heart, blood, and blood vessels are parts of your respiratory and circulatory systems. Working together, the parts of the systems get needed oxygen from the air to all parts of your body and return your gaseous wastes to the air. Added to all your other parts and systems, they make one larger living system, namely, you! If any part of you doesn't work well, the rest of you may feel sick. It may take a physician to help get your systems running well again.

If the breakdown of any major part in a human system is so severe that the other organs or body parts can't do their jobs properly, the person may die. And so it is with the living community of plants and animals. These are organisms that are only parts in larger working systems—ecosystems and the biosphere.

An ecosystem includes everything—the amount and intensity of the sun's rays (photons); the air and water with their varying temperatures, gases, and chemicals; the rocks and soil with their varying temperatures, depths, hardness, and permeability; all the living organisms and dead materials. Everything that is in an ecosystem is part of that ecosystem.

Whether an ecosystem is in a habitat described as desert, as grassland, as evergreen forest, as deciduous or hardwood forest, as ocean, sea, or high mountain, as Arctic iceland or tundra, as lake, river, pond, or fishbowl, the ecologist tries his best to look closely, observing, examining, and learning about everything within the boundaries of the place he has decided to study. He wants to learn how the ecosystem functions—how all the things in this one place work together and affect each other. "In what ways is this

Weather station at the Hubbard Brook U.S. Forest Service Station

ecosystem changing?" "Is this life system balanced in a climax stage so that everything keeps living and appears to stay the same?" Or, "Is this system dying or dead?" the ecologist asks himself.

To learn how an ecosystem is changing, the ecologist must know its past history as well as its present state. Then he can predict its future.

As the ecologists looked at the Hubbard Brook watershed, many questions filled their curious minds: What was the forest, the weather, the lake and the soil like long ago and in the more recent past? What do the streams carry away with them? What plants and animals used to live here? Are the same organisms here now? Did the different groups of people that have used this area make permanent or impermanent changes?

Watching the leaves quiver, hearing their rustling, rainlike sound, the ecologists wondered what was happening in the forest today. What changes, if any, were taking place in the air, the soil, the streams, the lake, the plant cover, and the animals that might cause the environmental conditions to alter the plants and animals that could exist here?

To see what was happening in this Northern hardwood forest now, what had happened in the past, and what might happen in the future Dr. Likens and Dr. Borman needed X-ray ecology eyes. They would have to see through things to what was happening. Questions and answers—finding causes and effects by recorded measurements and observations would give them X-ray vision into forest happenings.

The scientists would be able to find the answers to some of their questions. But it would take more than their two lifetimes to answer all the questions. Impatient, they wanted to know facts about the forest and see what was happening in a shorter time. It takes long daily hours of work to do the measuring, counting, and recording of data that would eventually answer the questions. Lots of bits of facts must be fitted together to tell the story of a "happening." Also, it takes lots of muscles and energy to collect the measurements. An ecologist may have to climb trees or mountains, wade up streams, or row across a lake to take measurements. These two men just didn't have the time and energy to do the whole job of learning what was happening in the Hubbard Brook ecosystem.

But they could learn a piece of what was happening. They would do what they could. Later, others could do more and the early pieces of information would help them.

Where to begin? The forest was complex, its parts interwoven like the threads of a colorful Navajo rug. And the ecologists wanted to see the overall patterns in the forest the way you see the pattern in a rug. To sharpen their thinking and to help their eyes see the pattern rather than individual threads, they kept in mind a diagram.

Ecologists study what is happening in a community, how one thing affects

—changes or doesn't change—something else. They may diagram this with arrows to show the action between the elements or parts of the environment. Only two arrows are needed in the diagram to show action, because all the action or changes in any environment can be classified into one of two groups or categories—energy or materials.

Energy is the ability to do work. As work is done, energy is changed to a less organized and usable form. The sun's rays give the earth its original life energy.

Plant leaves are the factories. Their green chlorophyll captures the sun's light energy and uses it to combine carbon and oxygen from carbon dioxide (CO_2) in the air with hydrogen (H) from water to create a sugar (glucose) that is stored in parts of the plant for future use. This process, photosynthesis, is a chemical process man has yet to understand completely and duplicate.

Plants use their own stored sugar for their own living activities. But there is a sugar surplus that animals can use after they eat the plant. By way of a plant and animal food chain, the stored energy from the sun is passed to human beings, keeping them alive, growing, mending, and reproducing. Extra energy is stored in our bodies as fat, ready to answer the energy needs of our bodies. When we run, jump, play the piano, or think, our body chemicals can change our stored energy—the fat—to other chemicals that give the quick energy needed by our muscles to do work, or the energy needed by the cells in our body to grow, mend, or perform their jobs.

The stored energy we give our automobiles is gasoline. When the supply of gasoline is gone from the tank, our car won't budge on the level unless we use our own energy and push it. An ecosystem needs food energy to keep it running, just as a car needs gasoline.

Every ecosystem has (1) energy stored for future use, (2) energy that is changing its form, and (3) energy that is being used to do a job. In the process or act of being used or changing form, some energy is changed into heat and rises into the air, lost for future use on earth. Energy and its ability to change forms helps people to jump, cars to go, and ecosystems to function.

The material that makes up all life is limited or finite. Atoms that join together to make carbon dioxide, nitrogen, oxygen, water, calcium phosphate, and other materials upon which plant and animal life depend are limited in number.

All the materials of the earth can be found in either gaseous, solid, or liquid form in the atmosphere, or on and in the soil and earth. The same materials move around or cycle from place to place or from form to form in an endless chain. Without the processes to build up and tear down, thus changing forms, all the elements would get tied up in trees, animals, rocks, and clouds and stay there permanently. Life would be a statue rather than a motion picture.

Parts of a rock dissolve in the stream water and enter a plant by its roots to become part of a tree, perhaps an acorn that some busy squirrel eats. A fox makes a meal of squirrel and the phosphorus from the rock now helps the fox live. Perhaps fox is caught in a trap and dies. The bacteria, insects, and other soil creatures help move that "foxy piece of rock" into themselves or back into the soil for a new plant to use.

Earth's materials move around from one place to another as if they were loaded into boxcars on a toy railroad track traveling from one stop to another, where some elements get off and other elements get on. Eventually the boxcars return to their starting point, having completed a full circle and made a system for moving materials. This endless chain is like your respiratory or circulatory system.

You can compare earth materials to bricks or a child's building blocks. One time the blocks may form or shape a castle. Torn down, the same blocks can be used again for a bridge. Torn down repeatedly, they may in turn become a wall, a tower, or eventually another castle. The chemicals found in our biosphere cycle in a similar manner. One day materials may be part of a cloud, another day part of a river, an ocean, a tiny plant in the ocean, a small fish, a tuna, or you who ate the tuna fish. You perspire and a bit of heat leaves your skin as it helps the water droplets to evaporate, returning to the air and a cloud.

Energy makes it possible for the earth's materials to cycle and change form. Energy pays the price for changing the form of materials. Whenever a frog turns into Prince Charming, some energy is lost into the atmosphere as heat.

To get a better idea of this magical change of forms, let's follow a fly. Buzzing about a frog, fly gets stuck on frog's long tongue and is soon being changed by frog's stomach juices into frog. But frog doesn't get all the energy that fly had originally. Fly had used some of its energy to change grass into fly and to live. The stored energy left in fly is passed on to frog, minus the energy needed to break fly down into building blocks that could become frog.

You may eat cereals and beef, but you don't look like a cornflake or a steak. Your body juices digest these nutrients, breaking them down into small molecules. Your stored energy makes it possible for your body to reassemble the small bits of chemicals into you.

Materials changing form with the help of food energy is the basis for food chains—an important "happening" in any ecosystem. The grasshopper eating grass is in turn eaten by a frog who is consumed by a snake who is taken by a hawk that loses out to a bobcat who is trapped by man and becomes

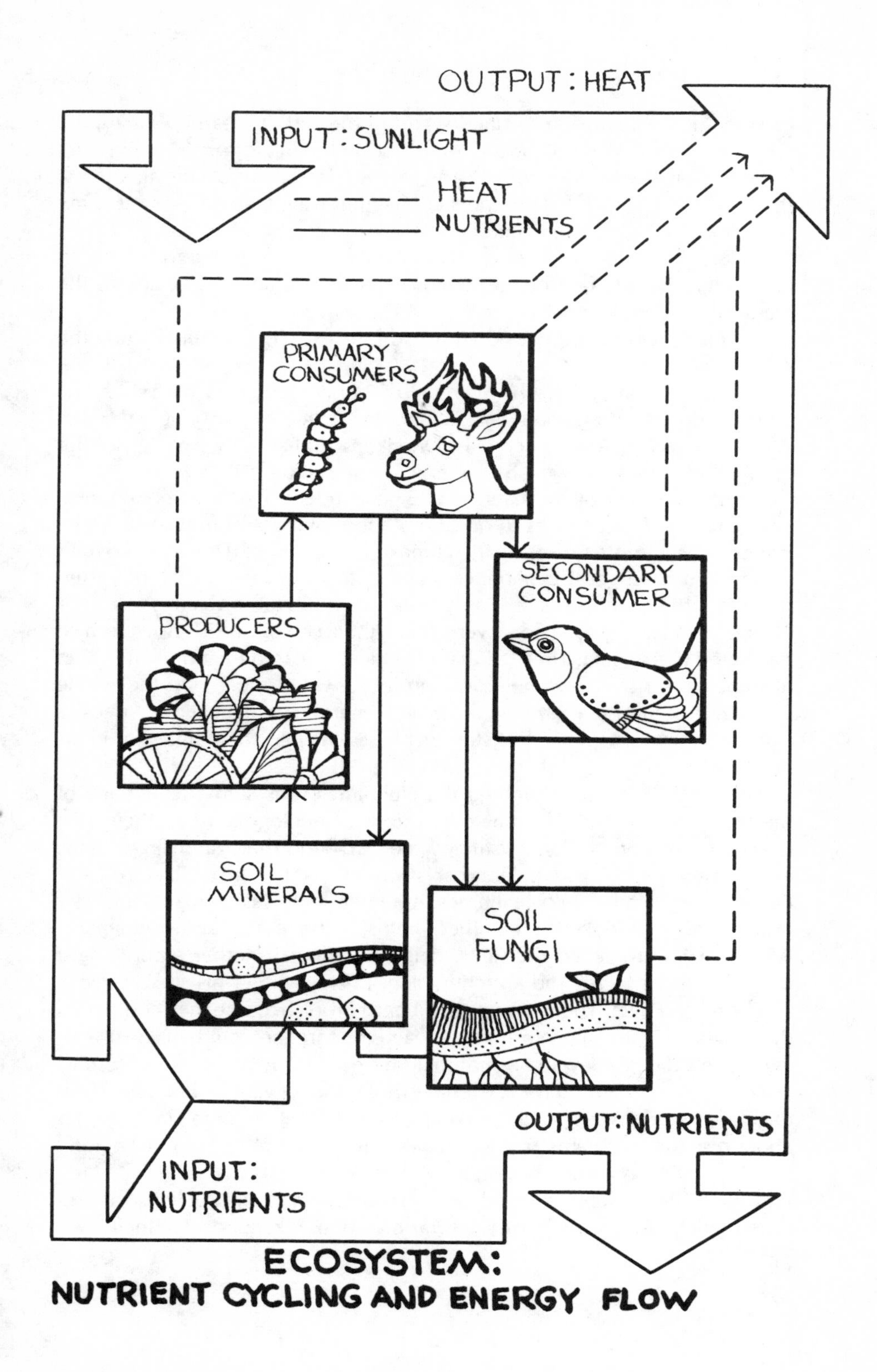

ECOSYSTEM:
NUTRIENT CYCLING AND ENERGY FLOW

carrion, or dead animal material, for part of the earth's clean-up squad, the vultures. Each link in this or any other food chain is forged by energy.

With their flow chart of energy arrows and material, or chemical, arrows, the ecologists could follow the action—the way materials and energy moved in their ecosystem study.

Where does one start piecing a forest ecosystem puzzle together? As with any picture puzzle, put the pieces you recognize together first, and as the picture grows you recognize more pieces.

Dr. Herbert Borman, the botanist and forest ecologist, would study the plants.

Dr. Gene Likens, the freshwater ecologist or limnologist, would study the streams, ponds, lakes, and rivers. A limnologist studies all about water that is not salty. As an aquatic ecologist Dr. Likens studied salty waters too. But at Hubbard Brook only fresh waters were present.

Both men were college teachers and had students who wanted to tackle problems and find answers to questions about plants and fresh water. The professors had more questions than time to find answers. They wanted their students to have good experience learning to do research that interested them, so the students helped form questions and gather data.

The principal investigators were more than ecologists. They were also dedicated to teaching. They felt that individual research freedom—freedom to choose and develop one's own project—would most help the whole study and at the same time give the best in graduate education. After the students assembled their data, the professors helped them analyze, interpret, and explain the facts they had gathered.

Other scientists learned about the Hubbard Brook study. New parts of the puzzle were worked on as other kinds of ecologists asked their own questions. The ornithologists studied the birds and then, studying insects, acted as entomologists. A paleobotanist was invited to core the lake bed and delve into the plants of ancient times. A herpetologist selected a salamander problem but also looked at the other "herps"—the reptiles and amphibians. A mammalogist studied the furry, hairy mammals. Another entomologist identified the insects. And an ichthyologist fished to get his specimens.

The researchers liked working at Hubbard Brook because they could pool their data. By sharing information, each researcher could make use of everyone's data to develop or compare his own study and his own results.

At any time of the day or evening researchers living at Pleasant View might be found on the porch working—reading, writing, or talking together about research problems. The porch was also a fine place for relaxing and chatting with the friends or family who came to visit.

Some of the student researchers worked on research problems that resulted in a master's thesis or doctoral dissertation required for their own

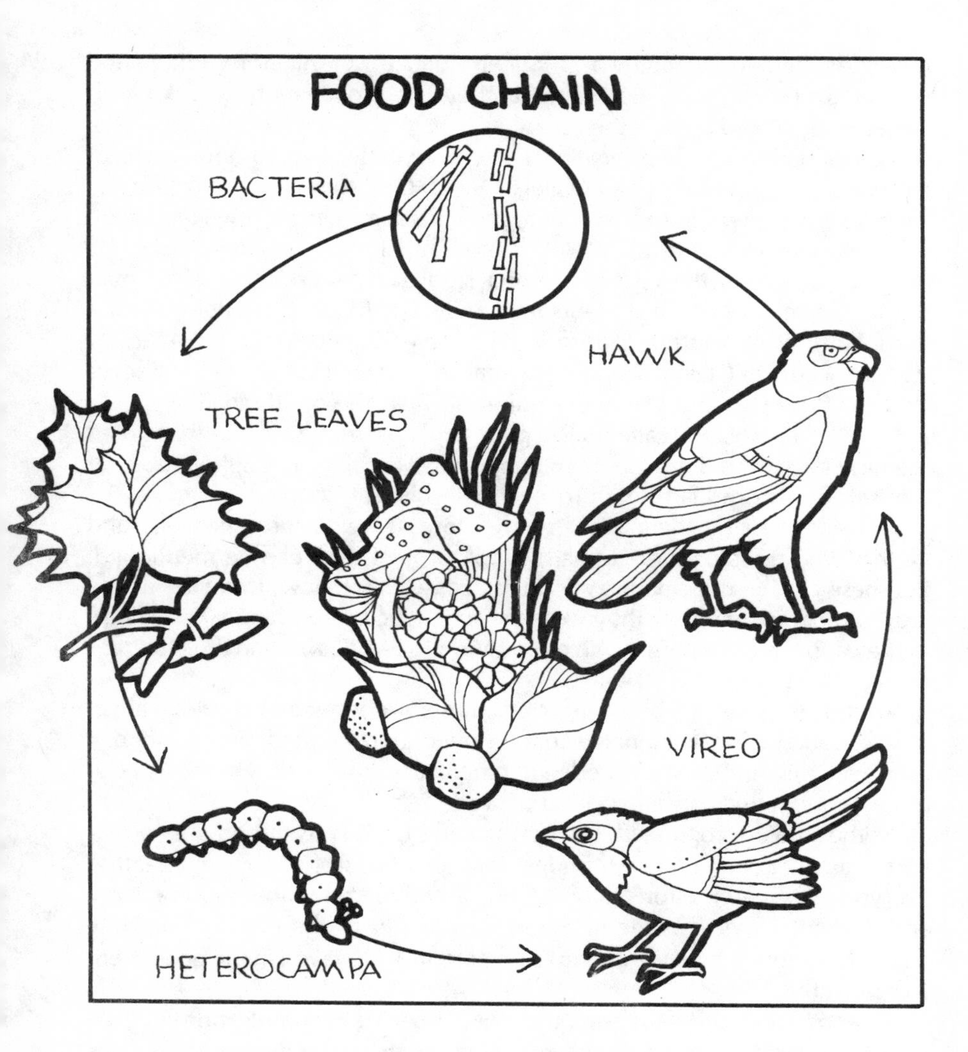

advanced college degrees. Other students gathered data for the principal investigators' research projects. The researchers used first names. Where you might become confused by three Daves and three Toms or misidentify people, last names have been added.

Dr. F. Herbert Borman had students and assistants—Bob Muller, Peter Marks, Tink, Patsy, and Don—to help piece the ecosystem puzzle together.

Some of Dr. Gene Likens' students from Cornell University were Dave Gerhardt, Dave Mazsa, Penny, Joe, Jim Gosz, and Tom Burton. Another Tom, Tom Baker, a Cornell undergraduate student, was hired by the ornithologists. Bernard became an Evergreen College, Washington, student and worked for Dr. Likens and other researchers. He did a variety of jack-of-all-trades jobs, as did some other students.

Dr. Richard T. Holmes, called Dick, was within a two-hour drive of Hubbard Brook at Dartmouth College, New Hampshire. Dr. Frank Sturges, from Beaver College in Pennsylvania, spent his summers in New Hampshire with his wife, Pat, and daughters, Sheryl and Karen. Helping these two ornithologists with the bird and insect studies, or working on their own studies, were Dartmouth students Ian Law, Craig Black, Gary Potter, and a third Tom, Tom Sherry. A third Dave, Dave Zumeta, was a Haverford College student. Dorothy Willwerth, called Dot or Dottie, was a Beaver student. Both Dot and Dave were hired to help the ornithologists.

Dr. William Reiners, called Bill, a plant ecologist from Dartmouth, studied the new growth in the experimental cut areas and hired people already at the Brook or from Dartmouth to help with his leaf counts.

Needless to say, there were many more students, professionals, and visitors who peopled the Hubbard Brook project than can be mentioned. But these are the principal players in the pages that follow. Knowing where they came from and why they were there may help you identify individuals as they appear in the scenes at Pleasant View, Mirror Lake, and the Hubbard Brook Forest.

Within ten years Hubbard Brook became a cooperative ecological research center. The National Science Foundation granted money to pay some salaries and buy needed equipment and materials for the special projects submitted to them and approved.

As the studies progressed, Dr. Borman and Dr. Likens turned their attention to an energy and nutrient budget for the entire system, pulling together everyone's research efforts. Now they wanted to know how much energy and nutrient material came into and moved out of the ecosystem. They wanted to know where the energy and material that stayed in the ecosystem were located.

An ecosystem budget is something like a bank account. If more money comes in than goes out, your savings account grows. If more money goes out than comes in, you may go bankrupt and your account dies. If the same money that goes out comes in, your account is stabilized and stays the same. Would the ecologists find the ecosystem being studied at Hubbard Brook mature and stabilized in a climax condition, in a growing stage, or dying? Energy and material budgets should tell the answer.

3

THE OLD FARMHOUSE

Where to put all the people needed to piece the ecosystem puzzle together was a problem solved by renting a large historic farmhouse. Pleasant View was the summer home for the researchers. New arrivals slowly eased their cars up the narrow, blacktopped lane into a tire-rutted dirt drive. Before them rose a huge, three-and-a-half-story white clapboard house. The long, wide porch beckoned them to find a chair, rock, and enjoy the pleasant view of the White Mountains.

Two hundred years old in parts, the house had its own unique history. Hidden plates for counterfeit money, an underground railroad station for escaping slaves, tavern, resort, rooming house, restaurant, tourist home, family home, and research station were all chapters of its past. The home had been in Henrietta's family for a hundred years. She rented it to Dr. Likens and Dr. Borman and in a motherly way cared for "her boys," as she called the young researchers. Her home was a short distance away, and she frequently dropped in to leave a sample of her latest baking, a cashed check, laundry, or an invitation to her famous turkey dinner.

Indeed, Pleasant View was a pleasant place to be. The new fifty-year-old forest softened the rounded humps of the mountains. Within the wide circle of mature and sapling white pines, balsam fir, white birch, and aspen, tall green grasses were dabbed with spots of purple vetch, red paintbrush, and orange filaree. A broad patch of grass was mowed for a lawn in front of the house. Two one-hundred-year-old trees, an oak and a maple shaded the front yard, the flagpole, and a camp trailer. The aspen leaves with their

Pleasant View

The view from Pleasant View's front porch

twisted stems moved with the slightest air movement, retaining their coolness.

In the evening, from the porch, researchers watched the aerial display. Swallows dipped for their dinner. Bats darted after insects and hid their nesting young between the wall of the old house and the attached garage. Their squeaky cries mystified and stirred the researchers to investigate.

As the sun set in the west behind the house, the darkness brought fireflies, stars, and a waxing or waning moon over the field.

Inside, the house had been modernized through the years. Seven fireplaces were walled in and replaced by a basement oil furnace. An oil burner heated the living room in the winter. And two gas stoves with trash burners in the kitchen cooked meals and took the chill off cool mornings and rainy days.

Kerosene lamps had been replaced by electric lights in 1920, and the outhouse was abandoned for a downstairs bath in 1950. Later an upstairs bath was added.

The front door opened into a large entryway and a flight of stairs that led to numerous bedrooms. Five downstairs doorways led to the parlor, two dining rooms, the bath, and two attached bedrooms. The busy kitchen was off the dining rooms. The back porch was turned into a lab and looked out on a forty-foot trailer lab.

The interior of the house was a strange mixture of antique furniture and recent research. The parlor, with gray paint, faded red-flowered wallpaper, and a linoleum carpet over prized wide floorboards, was the relaxing room. Here researchers read, played cards or checkers, or made music on the piano, violin, and flute. They sewed, wove, knitted, conversed, and listened.

The twin dining rooms had once served tourists meals. Now they held research clutter. Family pictures and paintings decorated the walls, while a china closet still enclosed Henrietta's glassware and dishes. But the yellow and pink plastic tablecloths covering two sturdy oak tables were never set with the pretty dishes or flower centerpieces—they were littered with research paraphernalia. Collecting bottles, cotton wads, piles of papers, files of records, journals stacked high, binoculars, typewriters, calculating machines, reprints, microscopes, scales, glass vials, tape recorders, maps, charts, index card files, and empty fruit cans all claimed their places in the dining rooms.

The kitchen was another place where the crews could socialize. Two stoves lined one wall. A sink and small counter fitted one side of the dining doorway, a dish hutch the other side. The middle of the room was filled by two long tables. A refrigerator and phone table took up a remaining wall. A small pantry off the kitchen held pots and pans along with researchers' grocery sacks and boxes, all labeled with big black letters: TB, DM, DZ, DH, TS, FS, etc. Initialing everything was the way the researchers identified their own materials. Refrigerators held containers with the same black letters.

How did many people working under the grants of several principal investigators live in one house with one kitchen and two baths? With difficulty and a sense of humor!

One cook would have had an impossible job, never knowing how many were coming to a meal. Researchers' schedules all differed. The number of invited scientific groups with pup tents in the fields changed too. So everyone took care of his own meals. A few people with compatible schedules joined forces to prepare, cook, eat and clean up. If a researcher's stomach growled and the kitchen was empty too, that was a good time to fix dinner. If the kitchen was full, he would just have to wait for a space and a pan.

Although this was not intentional communal living, it sometimes appeared to be. The researchers suffered some of the problems of such living groups. Lots of people make lots of trash—getting the trash to the local dump was a problem.

Everyone took his turn at nightly kitchen clean-up jobs. Muddy field boots made daily hall and stair sweeping a goal. Before the summer work closed, everyone joined in one grand housecleaning day.

Bathrooms were another problem. Waiting turns was not always so easy as waiting to use the kitchen. Everyone scrubbed out his own bathtub ring and tried to keep the floor dry. When the well was very low during a drought, people swam in the lake to get clean. Most of them swam in the lake every day anyway, so this was not an inconvenience. Henrietta solved the water problems by drilling a new well for her "boys and girls." But a new well didn't help the cities downstream that depended on the mountain river waters. We all take water for granted until we don't have it. Maybe the tree cutting experiments would show us ways to keep an even amount of water flowing down the rivers all year.

When it rained, more people stayed in the house and caught up with their bookwork and record-keeping. Once it rained almost solidly for four weeks. But the young, active minds could not be dulled by indoor monotony. The researchers invented. The kitchen was often the scene of their creations.

Sitting in the back dining room, Dave Z., an undergraduate student, rocked and read to Bernard, Dr. Borman's son, who listened intently to a recipe for coffee cake.

"Heh, that sounds good. I wonder how much that costs to make? Probably about the same as half a cake. Look in our book and see," Dave said.

Sheryl, daughter of a resident scientist, walked over and peeked at the figures in their spiral notebook that Bernard was examining closely. All the amounts of the ingredients were in decimals and grams. There were three recipes for the same coffee cake with only slight differences in the amounts of the ingredients. Next to each ingredient was its cost: 2¢, 5¢, etc. These were the most scientific cooks Sheryl had ever seen. They made their cooking an experimental activity rather than a job or an art.

"What's that good aroma coming from the kitchen?" Sheryl asked.

"Our number 3 coffee cake. We'll let you sample it when it's done," Bernard offered.

Dave kept rocking and reading. Bernard told him whether a recipe sounded good.

"Hey, you really like to cook, don't you?" Sheryl said.

"Got to do something," Bernard quickly replied.

This was their first cooking year. They often discussed recipes and cooking. They didn't fit the stereotypes of young men or scientists. They shared a common interest with their mothers and grandmothers.

While everyone ate the coffee cake, Bernard fingered through Peterson's bird guide. The researchers picked up field guides and keys to identifying all sorts of natural things—they thumbed through them the way most people look through a magazine or read a novel.

Karen, Sheryl's sister, joined the group. "Let's play the 'What Bird Is It?' game," she said between munches of cake. "Like, what bird is a Halloween bird that plays dodge ball?" Karen invented a new game for the group.

"We give up," Sheryl said.

"A masked duck," Karen answered.

"Oh no—" Dave moaned.

Dave M., a biology student, popped in for a break from the porch lab and got the drift of the game. "What about a party in a pasture bird?"

Quickly bird names flitted through their heads. Robin, bluebird, crow—nothing seemed to fit that description.

"Meadowlark," Karen answered.

"Right!" Dave congratulated her.

Glancing up from his book, Bernard offered, "A large clear-stream bird."

"Shearwater," Karen responded, much to Bernard's surprise.

"Almost. The greater shearwater," he corrected her.

"The kitten bird," Dot called from her caterpillar table.

That was easy. They all called at once, "The catbird."

Television and radio reception were very poor. Tape recorders and records brought classical music and the current rock sounds to the farmhouse. Piano music floated from the living room windows on warm evenings. Fiddlers and guitarists filled the house or the porch with lively country music.

Jokes focused on things that wouldn't hurt people's feelings. One man was teased about his "cold blood," since he was always cold and needed his heavy jacket. Dave's weekly casserole was inspected nightly for the new ingredient added each day. They all got along remarkably well, just like a family whose members liked and respected each other. Something usually was happening—it was never dull.

Sunny days brought timeless hours. The world seemed to be this one place. Time stood still. In free moments people sunned, hiked, picked berries, hunted antique bottles, watched birds and dogs.

Many pets came and went. Aob, a boa constrictor, had no snake-sitter at home. She had had to come along. Her cage was kept in the garage, and Frank, an ornithologist, moused for her.

The animal behaviorists discovered that a male and a female dog got along better than did two females or two males. When a new dog arrived, the first question was always, "Male or female?"

Donda, Frank's boxer dog, gave lessons in territorial claims and defense. Whenever a new dog arrived on the scene, she had to get acquainted. The dogs learned either to play together or to stay in their own territory, which they defended with growls, barks, and threatening positions.

The older dogs put up with the capers of puppies. They taught them the rules of being a canine. Rick's little red setter learned quickly to give up when attacked by a big dog. He rolled on his back and bared his throat to his attacker. He also learned to hide in small holes in the bushes and under cars.

A retriever played an outstanding game of frisbee. She ran to catch the flying disk, caught it in her teeth, and returned it to her master. Time and time again she entertained the audience on the porch with her catching prowess.

Baseball, catch, badminton, and volleyball were the before- and after-dinner sports.

The first volleyball net was too low. People recoiled from the attacks of strong players. So Bernard made tall poles from two saplings and sunk them securely in the ground. An official-sized net was stretched between the poles, and boundary lines were roped off. Much better games followed.

As varied and different as the group was in appearance, personality, likes, and dislikes, they all seemed to really like the outdoors. On a weekend many would climb a mountain. Some tried to climb them all in one summer.

As a group, the researchers, like young people everywhere, had a wide range of individual interests and varied talents. Most important, they exercised their talents and interests, always actively involved in doing something. No one moped around, or wondered what to do. They were healthy, strong, and energetic.

Tom Baker, the insect man, kept his legs and lungs fit for cross-country racing by running two to five miles a day. A few nights a week he played the piano in a local restaurant.

A Yale botany student named Tink swam around the lake regularly. He read *Stalking the Wild Asparagus* and did his own hunting and preparation of edible roots, seeds, and plants from the field. He also played in the Naval Reserve Band. His flute-playing inspired Karen to choose that instrument to play in school.

After the day's bird-watching chores, Ian played the piano or fiddled for a hoedown with Tom S., a fellow Dartmouth student. Sometimes he sketched the animals and plants around him or pictured the funny doings of researchers.

Even though the researchers were strongly individual in their pursuit of interests and had their own ideas about lots of things, each was content to let the other fellow do his own thing if it didn't interfere with their own activities.

Only an occasional helper had a reputation for crawling off into the grass, lost from view and a job assignment. If helpers didn't like to work hard, they quit or didn't come back. To most of them, the work was what they would choose to do. So the hours spent working were hours living, not waiting to live.

A more likable group of young people would be hard to find. The future rested in capable hands. All in their own ways became aware of earth's population and environment problems. Each wanted to help. They were preparing themselves to help recognize and solve environmental problems.

Population pressures at Pleasant View

They were ready to make sacrifices. Several couples gave up their desire for many children and planned for one or two. Others planned all or partly adopted families. Still others decided to have no children of their own. They would give their time to other people's children and devote their energies toward making the earth a better home for all the earth's family members.

Projects grew. The number of people grew too. Pleasant View had its own population crunch. Something had to give. Another house was rented. It was christened PIP (Principal Investigator's Pad) by the research assistants. Then the birders migrated to a "birdhouse" down the road.

Increasing numbers of researchers, assistants, and visiting scientists created new problems. The crowding was relieved by new rules, a new well, tents, a trailer, and more house rentals.

4

INPUT AND OUTPUT

Interested family, friends, and visiting scientists were given guided tours of the forest experiments. Sometimes a researcher took a "busman's holiday" to see what new things were happening in other workers' projects.

Imagine yourself going along on one such tour to see the water input and output measuring equipment. The invisible chemicals (solutes) and larger materials (particulates) are measured in the water that comes into the system (input) and goes out of the system (output).

When you are riding in the car whose destination is Watershed 2, the clear-cut, it is hard to believe the lush vegetation of the broad-leaved hardwoods with their intense green. The world is a technicolor film taken through a green filter.

At a sharp turn, a small waterfall coming over a miniature cement dam appears to the left of the road. It is one of the nine weirs on the drainage basin. The low, foot-thick cement wall forms a three-sided dam. You can see a small stream flowing into a shallow pool over the rock and cement bed behind the dam. Some water is passing through the V-notch centered in the front wall of the dam. Except for creating a pleasant place for water striders, green frogs, and diving beetles, it seems a useless pond.

Next to a side wall, a five-foot-square guardhouse rises eight feet tall. Any minute you expect a sentry to rush from its narrow closed door. None will, because this gray blockhouse protects the measuring instruments that keep a continuous record of the amount of water that flows through the V-shaped cut in the dam. Five one-inch round holes in the side wall allow water to flow into the floorless house. The water is always the same level inside the house as in the pond. Since water "seeks" its own level, the protected instruments measure and record the level of the pond by measuring the water level inside the house. The V-notch allows the water to leave the pond gradually and be measured as it flows out. By measuring the water in the pond and the amount running out, scientists can figure how much water is running off the whole Hubbard Brook drainage basin. They measure the amounts of chemicals in the runoff too. All the water that enters this drainage basin leaves by way of small streams like this one, which can be measured.

Imagine yourself standing in a shower with the water running and holding a funnel. All the water that falls on the inside of the funnel will drain down and out the hole, out of the basin.

The slanting, hard rocks under the soil act like the sides of your funnel, directing the flow of underground water to surface streams. Extra surface water that can't be absorbed fast enough by the soil or plants cuts streambeds as it flows down a slope. Surface and underground waters, then, come together in this stream and pass through the weir just as water runs from the end of the imaginary funnel. This stream drops down the hillside to join other streams. These, in turn, join to make Hubbard Brook, the big stream used for swimming and fishing. The semicircling slopes of the mountainsides act like the sides of your funnel. The weir allows the scientist to measure more accurately the amount of water that flows out of the ecosystem.

While instruments at the weir record water output, water gauges near the weather stations measure the input of water into this drainage system from all forms of water—rain, snow, sleet, hail, dew. With accurate input and output measurements, researchers can figure how much water is used or stored in the basin. Then when trees, which use water, are cut, foresters can predict what will happen to water levels of streams below the cut area.

In heavy rains more water falls than the ground can absorb. Extra water runs off as surface water, swelling the streams and moving soil and rock debris as it flows toward the ocean. Slower moving water creates more groundwater which can keep supplying rivers and streams during dry as well as rainy spells. If we don't take proper care of our watersheds, cities far away from the forests may find themselves with floods from too much run-off water or drought from lack of groundwater.

Hubbard Brook experiments may show that clear-cutting a certain proportion of trees may cause quicker melting of snow cover in the spring and more water in the streams. If there's a drought, perhaps cutting some trees would leave more water in the soil, since tree leaves transpire—give off to the air—many pounds of water. Experimenters have to try different things,

The amount of water leaving the watershed is recorded at the weir

keep accurate records, and analyze to figure out what their numbers, or data, mean.

Graduate assistants have helped take the input and output data. Frequently, they have been chemistry majors as undergraduates, able to do the chemical analysis of the water and particulate matter—materials in the water that can settle to the bottom of the settling basins. First, they must discover what materials were in this ecosystem. Second, they must discover the amounts of materials that occur over a period of time—weeks, months, years, decades, centuries.

Energy and materials may enter, stay, pass through, or escape from an ecosystem. Chemical tests on the water entering and leaving the ecosystem would enable the researchers to learn what happened to the water as it passed through the ecosystem. The water could dissolve materials as it made its way down the slopes. Or the plants and animals could take materials out of the water. To estimate accurately water and chemical input and output was their main problem.

The Forest Service measured the amount of water output by placing a network of weirs across each small stream that left the ecosystem study area. These V-notched weirs measured the changing flow of water.

In big storms and downpours, when water rushes out over the top of these weirs, Forest Service flumes record the height of the high water. Measurements recorded in the cement blockhouse show how high the water can get.

One assistant's job has been to collect water samples each week and analyze them for the same chemicals that have been checked in the weather station (input) water: Ca, Mg, Na, K, Al, NH_4, Cl, NO_3, SO_4, HCO_3, and SiO_2. The amounts of water and chemicals then have been fed into a computer at Dartmouth College. The computer took the Forest Service's measurements for the volume (V) of stream flow (how much water left the ecosystem) plus the concentration (C) of chemicals recorded during the same sampling period. The resulting figures showed the amount of chemicals lost from the ecosystem in kilograms per hectare (K/h): $C \times V = K/h$.

But not everything in the pond is a solute. The researchers have had to figure out how to measure the heavier things—the solid stuff at the bottom of the pool, or particulate matter. The organic material—parts of plants and animals that were alive at one time—and the inorganic material—rocks and soil, materials that have never been alive—must be measured too.

This quiet pool is a settling basin where particles can sink to the bottom. The weir seems like an oversized outdoor bathtub. There is a pipe at the bottom of the cement basin and a plug that can be pulled to empty the basin of water. The water can be drained from the basin through nylon mesh bags. What remains in the basin can be sorted into two piles, one organic and one

Forest Service takes regular input readings

inorganic. In all stages of decay are wood, twigs, leaves, bark, fruit, bud scales, and invertebrate animals. While in the inorganic pile are all sorts and sizes of cobbles, pebbles, rocks, weathered quartz, sand, and mica. If something is large, it is weighed right on the spot with a Chatillond spring balance. If an item is small, it can be taken to the indoor lab where a technician records its dry weight. A mathematical formula is used to calculate the annual output of larger materials from the ecosystem.

Knowing the amount of organic material passing out of the ecosystem enables the researchers to estimate the energy loss from this matter and to predict future losses.

Since weirs are only half the story, visitors must go up the road, hike to a weather station, and look at the input measuring equipment.

At fifteen miles an hour the car seems to race on the one-lane, curvy dirt road. Sharp eyes will glimpse birds or squirrels along the edge. In ten minutes the car pulls over to the bank, leaving room for another car to squeeze past.

Loop binoculars around your neck and glance up from the road to a clear view of a slice of hillside, barren of green trees. The ridge above the cut area etches a sharp outline against the clear blue sky. The gray-white bareness is startling. A stream flows down the center of the cut-over area and through a weir at its base.

From ridge to road cut, from one edge of the forest to the other, a stark graveyard of barkless trees lie like matchsticks from a box accidentally spilled. Ashen white and gray, the logs are in complete disarray. Long and short logs, one to three feet in diameter, crisscross, rising at odd angles from stacks three, four, and five logs deep.

The bark has completely peeled off, joining the other detritus, or dead plant parts, on the ground. The inner tree cores are left to weather gray like granite and marble tombstones. These are the skeletons of birch, beech, ash, and maple—all hardwoods. Look at one of the logs closely. Count its rings. If there are fifty, the tree was at least fifty years old when it was cut. Tree cells made during a rainy, fast-growth period are larger than those made during the dry parts of the year. The difference in cell size forms what appear to be rings. So each ring represents one year's growth here in the Northeast where there is only one dry season.

The smooth hard tree cores seem to grow larger as you scramble over them. Push yourself up on one log, walk its length, then step onto another log. Survey each log that crosses your path. Choose the one that angles up the slope toward your goal—the louvered white box on stilts in the middle of the log jam.

Tennis shoes cling to the dry, smooth, unsplintered trunk surfaces. Rubber cleated boots help a climber to stay out of the holes and crevices between logs. If you try to stay topside, jumping or leaping between logs in tennis shoes, you may slip on the smooth, rounded sides. Sliding feet hit the damp slippery sheet of bark under the log and keep slipping. Bark only partially decayed is wet and very slippery.

A slower, more careful pace pays unexpected rewards. If you see a quick movement between the logs, watch and wait. A mouse may jump from a gray crevice to the dark brown bark beneath your log. Coarse, yellowish-brown fur covers its back, blending into a dark brown strip that meets white fur along the side. The tail is very long. Mouse rises up on its hind feet, revealing its soft white belly. As suddenly as it appeared, the mouse jumps out of sight into a jumble of detritus under the logs. The jumping mouse, *Napaeozapus,* likes areas like this. There is a lot of protective covering, and seeds float in from the forest or have been scattered by the fallen trees. Food and protection—what more could a mouse ask? A jumping mouse can jump like a kangaroo, using its long tail for a three-point takeoff and landing. *Napaeozapus* moves by running and jumping. Jumping is a quicker way to cover ground and escape a pursuing predator.

The white box on stilts is a weather station with an anemometer for measuring wind, a rain gauge for measuring precipitation, and a maximum and minimum thermometer for measuring the highest and lowest air temperatures.

The rain gauge is a metal cylinder having an inverted cone-shaped top with an eight-inch-diameter opening. Water from the air rises along a ruler, or gauge, in the cylinder. A curious set of aluminum pennants hangs from a metal wire that encircles the opening of the gauge. The pennants move with only a slight gust of wind. These are good wind deflectors. The water collected must be only what falls straight down, not what is blown in from the sides.

The maximum and minimum thermometer hangs in the louvered white box. Metal bars rest on the ends of the mercury, which push the bars to the highest and lowest numbers as the temperature rises and falls. The data gatherers record the daily temperatures and then move the metal bars with a magnet to rest again on the mercury's two ends.

On top of the white box, twirling cups of the anemometer catch the breezes. Turning cups move a red stylus that marks an uneven red line on the paper attached to a turning drum inside the white box. The stylus continuously records the turning rate of the cups and consequently the force of the wind blowing the cups around and around.

It took three years before Dr. Likens felt that the weather measurements were accurate. Now Hubbard Brook has recorded over twelve years of daily facts. There is so much variation from year to year that it takes several years to get enough data for dependable averages. Now fairly correct pre-

Rain gauge: vanes deflect wind-blown water

dictions can be made with only small margins of error for rainfall and temperature. Weather data is now available to anyone working on a project in the study area.

The Forest Service has been measuring precipitation for many, many years. There is about one gauge for every 32 acres (13 hectares). They are located on each experimental plot and in the undisturbed forest. The Forest Service measurements have helped the ecologists a lot, but further measurements have been needed.

What chemicals are in the water that reaches the ground? These chemicals are available to life beneath the canopy. To make measurements, the ecologists set up collecting spots throughout their study areas. When it rains or storms, some poor graduate student must rush out to the forest to take water samples from each collecting site, getting drenched in the process.

Even up here away from the manufacturing and cities, researchers are finding heavier acid rains. The air currents take some of the pollutants away from their sources and spread them all over the countryside. Changes in the acidity of rain measurements are an indicator of more or less pollutants in the air. Just as a thermometer measures the warmth of the air, degree of acidity can measure air pollution. Twenty years of records tell us acidity has increased 100 percent in some places.

Will pollution continue to increase? People in the country who share the many manufactured products and modern conveniences produced near the cities find themselves sharing the unhealthy by-products too.

In a clear-cut it is hot. Layers of sweater and jacket come off. The slight air movement that lightly touches faces, drying and cooling them by evaporating perspiration, is appreciated.

A clear-cut "happening" will make you forget the heat. Tip your head backward and fasten your eyes on a piece of sky over the clearing. There, hanging in the air, upright as if it was standing on its tail, a sparrow hawk is batting its wings. Like a helicopter, it stays in one spot. Its strong, magnifying eyes probe the clearing for food. Through binoculars you can see its reddish cap surrounded by blue, the same slate blue that bars its wings. The male's rufous back and tail accent the blue. Its dark-black sideburns give it a proud, medieval look. In one smooth, quick motion, its long pointed wings fold close to its broad shoulders as it arches downward, diving like a free-falling missile. At the last moment feet thrust forward, wings spread to catch the air, and the sparrow hawk, with a furry mouse clutched hard in its talons, rises quickly to a high limb of a yellow birch beside the cut area. Was it that jumping mouse? This microenvironment suits the red-backed mouse and white-footed mouse too. Which has been prey for the predator?

Making a clearing changes the kinds of plants and animals that can live in an area. There's more cover for safety, more seeds and food for more mice. More mice mean more food for our sparrow hawk friends.

Halfway to the stream stop and peer at the side of a gray log. Poke a thin weed down a tiny but perfectly round neat hole. Near another hole just like it a long narrow beetle flashes its shiny metallic green and purple in the sun. Half an inch long, its six legs move it securely up the round log. The boring beetle is another member of the clear-cut community.

5

A PLANT TELLS

Water analysis can tell ecologists the condition of the atmosphere and streams. Plants can tell them what is happening to a stream too. Water was examined and measured at the weather station where it entered this ecosystem. It passed through the system by way of the small stream in the clear-cut and passed out of the system through the weir at the bottom of the ecosystem basin. Changes can occur as water moves down a hillside. Plants can sometimes "tell" what is happening to the water. Plants can also "tell" the stage of a clear-cut area's recovery.

The boring beetles, carpenter ants, and other insects have a lot of work ahead of them to open up the hardwood logs to fungi and other microorganisms. These will decay the unsightly mess and return raw materials to the soil for recycling into new plants. We can only guess how long it will take from what has been discovered in other places. Maybe thirty to fifty years may pass before this area could be naturally reforested by the same kinds of trees that were cut. Of course, other plants and trees will help cover the slope at first, changing growing conditions enough for a second group of trees, shrubs, and herbs to grow. The second group of plants would pave the way for a third group. After several stages of succeeding plant groups, conditions might be right for the original type of forest to sprout again and succeed. "Succession" is the word botanists use to describe these changing types of plants in one place. When an area stops changing and can stay the same way for a hundred years or more, botanists say the area has reached its "climax vegetation."

Lightning fires, drastic weather changes, volcanic eruptions, and other natural events can cause change too. Man is not the only factor affecting the environment.

Normally a cut forest will have root and stump sprouting the first year. But since the researchers are experimenting in this outdoor laboratory, they have killed the new growth chemically for a few years. They do here what can't be done indoors or might not be tried on commercial cuts. They are trying to learn what happens to the soil, plants, animals, water, and the microclimate when forests are clear-cut.

Usually in commercial lumbering loggers cut and haul many of the trees away. Roads are built and trucks enter the cut area. Many things happen at once. Here the cut trees are left on the ground so the scientists can study and learn what happens to stream flow when forests are clear-cut. Results won't be confused by other things happening at the same time. The researchers can compare the cut and uncut areas.

The experimenters picked two pieces of forest as nearly alike as possible. The cut area is the experiment. The uncut area is the "control" that tells what would have happened in the cut area if it hadn't been cut. After watching the two areas over a period of years, the experimenters will be able to make predictions of changes that will occur when similar areas are logged with this clear-cut method.

Hike through Watershed 4 and you'll discover strips of forest 160 feet wide next to strips of cut 80 feet wide, like the one you first visited. These are experiments with strip-cutting.

Predictions are only educated guesses. The more measurements taken and the more data gathered, the better the chance of an accurate prediction. That's why scientists usually qualify their predictions with "usually," "we think," "evidence indicates," "samples show." It is harder for scientists to make firm statements of fact, to say yes or no, when they must deal with opinions. They want to be accurate and stick to the facts, as far as they are known. Accurate facts are based on much research and data-gathering.

When scientists can't come up with instant answers, some people may feel betrayed and reject any or all scientific findings. They don't really understand how science and scientists work. They don't understand how the so-called "facts" are learned and how more information can modify or change the "facts." The more a person knows about how an experiment was done to get the "facts," the better his or her judgment can be in believing or questioning the results—the "facts."

Let's investigate the clear-cut stream. This area was cut in 1966, and sometimes to understand it the limnologist has to be a botanist too. A limnologist like Gene Likens studies freshwater plants and animals and the physical properties of water. But to be an ecologist, he may have to "turn his hat" a bit more and recall plant physiology from his botany classes.

We can do some of our own observing and make an ecological prediction.

Look closely at the water. Light-green plants edge the stream. The forest streams have these same mushy plants clustered along their banks. But those plants are more yellow-green than this blue-green mass. Does that difference mean anything? Some of the light-green mixes with the blue-green. This stream looks slimy compared to the other streams in the forest, under the trees. There are more blue-green than yellow-green plants in this clear-cut stream than in the forest waters.

The greens you see are named algae. There are two different kinds present. Some are called green and others blue-green algae (pond scum, to most people). They are two entirely different kinds of plant, as different as a pine tree and grass, even though they look very much alike to you. Here you are observing mostly blue-green algae, which grow very well in this stream and choke the steady flow of water.

Water must flow steadily and fairly rapidly or it will start looking like this, polluted. A faster flow rate adds oxygen, takes away decaying materials, and in general cleans up a stream or river.

Why are there more blue-green algae in this stream? Why do they grow better here in the clear-cut? Cutting the trees is the original cause. There is such a lot of plant life decaying or decomposing here. The saprophytes, such as some of the pretty fungi on the logs and stumps or the bacteria, too small for the naked eye to see, are busy with other decomposers like the boring beetle and small grubs. They all break up dead plant parts. Nutrients are being returned to the soil for recycling into new plant life. But there are no new plants to use the freed nutrients. New growth was killed as part of the experiment. The worms, centipedes, and insects that move soil, churning it like cake batter from the top to the bottom, haven't had time to do their job. So the rains wash extra nutrients, like the nitrates, down the hillside into rivulets which join this stream.

Scientists have been measuring nutrient content in the water for over ten years. A heavier load of nitrates is found here than in forest streams. The blue-green algae are clues or indicators that the stream is loaded with a certain kind of nutrient, the nitrates from the decaying plants.

Plants have tolerance limits. The idea of tolerance is complicated when you don't understand it and simple when you do. Some people can tolerate lots of strawberries. Other people can't. A person might tolerate a few strawberries, but break out in hives if he ate a lot. Desert plants can tolerate long rainless periods. Ferns can't tolerate rainless periods. Ferns will die in a desert where cacti manage to survive.

Blue-green algae can tolerate a lot more of this nitrate chemical in the water than plain green algae—the green algae won't grow well and the blue algae grows all right. Not only can the blue-green algae tolerate nitrates and grow, they grow better when they have nitrates. The green algae can't compete easily, so the needed nutrients that both species must have go into more blue-green algae growth. Instead of a balance between the two species you see mostly blue-green algae.

To our big rivers we add nutrients from our household and factory wastes. These wastes act like the extra nutrients from the decaying logs. More algae can grow. Then the Hudson, the Delaware, the Schuylkill, and the Potomac can all get polluted just like this little stream.

Some plants are good in streams. They are needed as food for the water animals like microscopic zooplankton, crayfish, and other fish. A balance of plants and animals helps make a clean, healthy river. But most of our big rivers aren't pure any more, and most of our small ones are getting poisoned and polluted.

If some plants are good, why aren't more even better? Too many plants make a stream sick, because eventually the plants die and sink to the bottom and then decay. The decaying plants free more nitrates and minerals in waters already overloaded with decaying sewage and other materials dumped into them. More nutrients enable more plants to grow—plants that will die, decay, and free even more nutrients for more plant growth.

The living plants multiply so rapidly in the water and the dead plants are so numerous that detritus builds up on the stream bed. The plants interfere with water flow. The stream slows down. Once the stream slows too much it can no longer keep itself clean. Decaying plants use oxygen, but don't make oxygen. Eventually decaying plants use up all the oxygen and crowd out the living plants and animals. Overpopulation of plants kills the stream or lake that at first joined with the sun, air, and seeds or spores to make new plant life. When there's no oxygen in a river, the living plants suffocate—they choke themselves to death.

The picture is not a pretty one. Plants need oxygen to decay quickly. When decaying plants use up all the oxygen, the whole stinking mess must just sit like thick, half-rotten soup, emitting the foul smells of slow anaerobic decay—decay without oxygen. The smoothly moving balanced cycle of constant and regulated change comes to a standstill. The nutrients are trapped. No more nutrients will be released to maintain a stream community. No new plants can grow without oxygen and nutrients.

We can make our own prediction from our own observations and the researched facts: mass plant suicide occurs with overpopulation of a water environment! This dramatic final scene of mass organism destruction and the death of an aquatic community is called eutrophication. That one long word, eutrophication, meaning the oversupply of nutrients to water and the overabundant growth of plants, tells an even longer tale.

Soil temperatures rise in the clearing where they are exposed directly to the sun. Yet it is pleasant inside the forest. The leaves on the trees make a great sunshade and their transpiration—release of water from leaves and evaporation by the sun—removes some of the heat from the air, cooling it. The forest is a good air conditioner on a hot summer day.

We move down the hillside and take our car back toward Pleasant View. Riding along, let's review what we found out at the weir, the weather station, and along the stream in the clear-cut: Water comes into the ecosystem, is measured at the weather station and analyzed for mineral content. Then moving downward toward an ocean, the water sinks into the ground or is used by a plant or animal. If a droplet doesn't evaporate into the air or become part of an underground stream, it moves along the surface, dissolving soil and chemicals, and pushing debris as it joins other droplets to make a stream. The droplet is measured and tested again at the weir and then continues its journey to the sea. Along its way to the ocean, water droplets may help one plant grow better than another, depending on the chemicals the droplet has dissolved. Eventually a droplet evaporates and falls again from a cloud as rain or snow—perhaps on Hubbard Brook, completing the endless chain.

6

BOTANISTS GET TO WORK

Principal Hubbard Brook investigators like Dr. Likens and Dr. Borman obtained their own grants of money from the National Science Foundation to cover research expenses. They asked other recognized research scientists to work under their "umbrella" and figure out sections of the Hubbard Brook ecological jigsaw puzzle. Their grant enabled them to give summer salaries to students working on master's and doctoral degrees. Students earned their degrees and at the same time worked on their chosen pieces of the Hubbard Brook ecosystem.

While Dr. Likens gave intensive study to the aquatic ecology of the study area, Dr. Borman, a botanist, became the terrestrial ecologist and looked at the plants. As plant taxonomist for the group, he named and identified the plants. Concentrating on the woody vegetation and the forest ecology, he listed all the species or kinds of plants present. Then he counted how many of each species grew in the study area. He chose Watershed 6 to sample. It was impossible to count every tree, shrub, and sapling in his sample study area. So he marked off a 25-meter-square grid and numbered each square in the grid.

If you numbered each square on a piece of graph paper, you would be making the same kind of chart as Dr. Borman did in the forest.

Next, he selected at random the squares to sample. Each square had the same chance to become a sample square. After the sample squares were selected, all the plants in each sample were counted and recorded by species name.

The part, or percentage, of the sample square covered by the canopy—

the portions of the sky covered by the top branches of the trees—was recorded too.

To figure out the standing crop or biomass of the woody plants, the diameter of each plant at breast height (four and a half feet off the ground), the height of the plant, and the surface area of each stem were measured.

In figuring out the nutrient content, or the chemicals present, and the energy content, a measured amount of each type of plant was burned in a bomb calorimeter. This measured the amount of heat energy given off. Then the ash was analyzed for chemicals. Mathematical formulas were used to figure the amount of energy in the plant biomass of each sample area and the amount of energy in the plant biomass for the whole study area. The nutrient content was expressed in kilograms per hectare, while the energy content was expressed in calories per hectare. The ecologist multiplied the number of kilograms or calories by the number of hectares in his study plot and the forest. In this way the total amount of mineral content and energy for the study area and the forest could be determined.

Plant density was reported for three elevational levels: lower (maximum density), mid-levels (less dense), and the highest levels (least dense).

Dr. Robert Whitaker sampled the major tree species. Cutting six of each species, he measured their dry weight. He hoped to get a base line against which to measure forest changes. One goal was to learn how much new biomass the major tree species created from the energy they received.

During the time Dr. Borman was determining the composition (what was there) and dynamics (how it worked) of the control watershed, he liked to get a bird's-eye view of the mountains and the basins by climbing favorite peaks that were in the Hubbard Brook basin, but out of the watershed area he studied.

He led expeditions and invited anyone around who wanted to hike. One afternoon his daughter, Becky, Dave Z., a birder, and Sheryl, a birder's daughter, joined an expedition to the top of Mt. Kineo.

As they left the road, the forest closed like a soundproof door behind them. A whitethroat's song, clear and loud a few steps before, was faint and soon lost as the climbers penetrated deeper into the woods. They immediately felt cooler. Entering the forest was like entering an air-conditioned room after a full blast of humid summer heat.

Here high quick trills and tinkling warbles rolled over each other again and again. The songster exercised his voice, ending on one high trill. Again, but closer, the beautiful full song filled the forest with melody. It must be a large bird to have such a large voice.

A "non-birder" would have scanned the treetops. But Dave pointed to the top of a small young bush. Straining their eyes, the girls finally spotted a tiny brown bird. When the song continued, Sheryl focused her binoculars, expecting to eliminate this speck of bird as the source of song. Surprisingly its throat vibrated with each trill. No more than four and a half inches from beak to tail tip, the winter wren had its stubby fanned-out tail cocked jauntily over its back. A long line over its eye resembled the line of a white eyebrow pencil. Its white belly was heavily barred with brown. Its rounded, dark-brown body shook with bursts of song. Finally the song ended. There was a silence and an emptiness in the forest. Bobbing its head, the winter wren flitted to a mossy tangle of stems and branch ends on the low damp rocks next to the stream.

Thunk, thunk, thunk—a downy woodpecker caught their ears and then their eyes. The black-and-white back and striking red spot on top of his head were very familiar. "Downies" make their homes in many places. They are widely distributed. They don't have to migrate like many insect-eating birds. Their steady supply of insect food is from the eggs and pupae formed in the fall and lying dormant through the cold winter in the bark of trees. They are not dependent on the warming spring's burst of new insects.

Windfall, the weakened limbs of trees blown to the ground, made treacherous footing as it lay wholly or partially hidden beneath the past fall's brown leaves. A cover of dried surface leaves hid the spongy, slippery layers of leaves holding winter and spring moisture.

Among established beech, sugar maple, birch, and occasional ash and hemlock, spindly saplings tried to grow and to add more leaves to the canopy above. Seeking a spot to bask in the sun's light, the young trees found the going rough. The canopy was already thick, crowding out newcomers. Very few young trees would get enough strength to enter the top layers. They wouldn't be able to make enough food, needed for growth, with only the filtered sunlight slipping through the leaves above them. What kinds of plants would grow in the new environment created by the shade? The success of the tall trees had changed the growing conditions for any newcomers. Though the future of the young trees was uncertain, their presence at the moment aided the hikers, who grabbed limbs to pull themselves up the hillside in their scramble to the top of Mt. Kineo.

Dr. Borman was a rapid, enthusiastic climber, always in the lead. Leaving the level forest floor, the expedition followed him up rocky stream beds blocked by giant wedges of granite rock to be skirted on the steep stream banks, through dense tangle of stunted spruce whose sharp needles and rough nubs dug into their clothing and scratched their hands as they covered their heads. Using the full weight of their bodies, they broke through the short, tight, flexible branches that filled the space between the spruce trees.

There weren't many clumps of needled evergreen trees in these mountains, but they really stuck together! The hikers couldn't see the mountain for the trees and almost missed the top. As they concentrated on each step, pressure toward the toes of their boots instead of the heels told them they were going down the other side. Dave climbed a tree to reconnoiter and reported they had indeed found the top. Down was two ways.

Dr. Borman, waiting for the group, had found a rocky outcrop. They all peered straight across the valley, as a bird would fly, to Mt. Mooselauke. Turning their heads 180 degrees, they could see another valley with its surrounding mountains—another basin.

It had been worth the climb, the scratches, and the three hours to conquer a mountain. The trees below were framed against a cloudless blue sky.

The trees they saw as they gazed across the valleys were not uncut, virgin forests. Except for a few protected acres, the virgin forests of Indian days were gone. The forests had been harvested several times since the pioneers had built their cabins, made their furniture, and burned their logs. These trees were a renewable resource. Handled properly, this forest would provide enjoyment for future peoples.

On the way down the mountain, Dr. Borman introduced the group to spruce gum, a hard resin from the spruce tree that became soft like chewing gum as the hikers heated it in their mouths. Turning the resin into gum required alternate chewing and spitting for about fifteen minutes. The taste was terrible. It was like the odor of lacquer or paint thinner. But after a quarter hour or more the strong taste was gone. The gum makers chewed and chewed until their jaws were sore and tired. The diversion of chewing helped keep their weakened legs and tired feet going downward. The climb down was almost as tricky as the climb up. Hidden limbs and logs beneath the slippery leaves on the steep trail caused a number of falls. After the six-hour hike, the group was glad to take the last climbing steps into the carryall.

Back at the farmhouse, Tink and Patsy, Yale botany students, came out lugging long bunches of limbs and twigs. They dumped them near a flimsy, wobbly camp table and went back upstairs to their second-floor bedrooms. Again the front screen door swung open as they lugged more branches between them and piled the wood on the first bunch. All the dried branches and leaves had been in the students' bedrooms under their beds! This was the only way they knew to keep the wood dry.

"That's the last of my batch," Patsy said.

"Mine too. Get the measuring tape out. I've got the cutters. We'll need the data sheet too," Tink directed. "Measure the diameter of each main branch and twig. Measure the length of the central branch, each branchlet and twig. Count and measure the leaves too."

Tink and Patsy busily pulled a measuring tape from its round capsule. As Patsy called out measurements, Tink recorded them on the chart securely fastened to his clipboard. After they measured lengths and diameters and counted the leaves, their information was plugged into a statistical formula that included a factor for error. The formula figured a total biomass for the tree they had cut down.

Your body has mass, otherwise you would float up into the air. Gravity pulls on that mass. A scale records a weight for your mass, all the substance that is your body. Squeeze your arm and feel some of your substance or mass. Iron shaped like your body would have a lot more mass than you do. There is less space between iron molecules than between your molecules. Iron is denser than you are, therefore it weighs more. Tink and Patsy were trying to figure out for different kinds of trees their masses or weights. Water-soaked wood weighs more than dry wood. Measuring wet wood would not give accurate weight. They would be weighing extra water as well as wood.

Next, Patsy and Tink put the measured tree pieces in the truck to take to the college for ashing, caloric measurement, and chemical analysis. The dry branches and leaves were burned in the special bomb calorimeter oven that measured heat. The heat measurement told them the amount of energy contained in the tree they had cut.

We defined energy as the ability to do work. A squirrel or chipmunk runs around getting food, burying nuts, and escaping predators. We can see that animals need energy to propel their activities. But a tree just stands in one place. What does it do? Why does it need energy? And how would it get its energy in the first place?

A tree does move, though it doesn't run around. It grows taller and wider, moving up and out. Granite monoliths have been cracked and split by the continual push of a seedling striving to grow and survive. Roots push down. Stems push up. Flowers, fruits, and seeds form. Cuts heal. Energy is needed to change the soil nutrients absorbed by plant roots into tree growth. "Blueprints" are put into the seed by its parents. Each tree grows according to the instructions in its seed. Different instructions are in each plant species. From the same materials very different-looking plants appear. The organism's blueprints are in its genes.

The sun is the builder that provides the energy to change the soil chemicals into different arrangements. This process, occurring in green plants, is called photosynthesis. The light from the sun strikes chlorophyll, the green part of a plant, and by complicated chemical reactions a plant stores or keeps the energy of the sunlight bound up in its parts. When the plant needs to do something, like growing, the sun's energy, stored away in stems, twigs, and tubers as food, is ready to help. Man's body cannot duplicate the green plant's process. Man, all other animals, and the nongreen plants could not live without green plants.

Some animals are carnivores—they eat only meat. Herbivores, like cows, eat only plants. And omnivores, like humans, can eat both meat and plants. But somewhere along a carnivore's food chain, an animal ate a plant and became a primary consumer for the secondary consumer that ate the plant eater.

The people in the world who eat only grains like rice, wheat, and barley are eating green plant storage bins for extra sugar. What a plant does not need for its own activities it stores in its leaves, stems, trunk, roots, fruits, and seeds. By measuring the mass of many trees and learning how much energy each tree released, the ecologists could estimate how much energy the forest produced and stored.

Stored energy made by plants and animals millions of years ago became today's coal and oil reserves. We burn them to get the energy to drive our cars and machinery and heat our homes. The reserves are finite. It is possible to use them all up. Eventually ecologists may be able to figure out how much energy forests, pastures, and farms produce. When mankind knows how much energy he can have to run the world indefinitely, he can pattern his activities to match his resources, keeping the endless chain of nature geared for survival on Planet Earth.

After the branches were taken to the lab, Tink jogged off to check root exudate measurement in the study plots. Plants change the chemicals in the ground around them. They give certain chemicals to the soil as well as take chemicals from the soil. These chemical changes can be measured.

On nice days Pleasant View's front porch was the scene of varied research activities. Dartmouth professor Bill R. and his crew of three busily picked leaves from branches and counted them. Picked in Watershed 2 (W2), a cut area, the leaves were used as a way of measuring new plant cover. No one dared interrupt Bill and his silent counters or they would have to start counting all over again.

Bob, a Yale graduate student, worked on a study of spring herbs that added more pieces of information to the Hubbard Brook ecosystem puzzle. He collected information about the herbs the same way Dr. Borman studied the woody plants. Bob randomly picked sample plots to study from the quadrat or grid pattern he outlined over his section of forest.

He worked out a list of the species present. He estimated the biomass production of one species, *Erythronium.* First, he clipped off above-ground parts of the small plants. He estimated their biomass. Then he collected its bulbets, or corms, from the soil. He took soil samples from his plot and spread the soil on large trays. Carefully he separated the soil from the corm. The porch and dining room tables were his laboratory. Bob put each part of the plant—leaf, fruit, flower, stem, corm—in a small aluminum cup and weighted it on the balance scale that sat on the buffet. He subtracted the

Pin cherry growth

cup's weight from each measurement. Eventually he added the weights together and knew about how much *Erythronium* biomass was present in each hectare of forest floor.

The Forest Service wanted to see what happened to water flow when more than one year passed without trees on a hillside. They clear-cut W2 and stump-sprayed to prevent root sprouting. After the Forest Service experiment, the pin cherry sprang up among the first sprouting plants in W2. This pioneer species in secondary succession interested graduate student Peter.

Like Bob, Peter took patches of forest soil from his sample plots and sorted them. He found a reservoir of pin cherry seeds that were just waiting to be exposed to the right environment of warm sun with no forest canopy. In those conditions the pin cherries sprouted quickly and grew rapidly. Pin cherries didn't grow in a forest. So how could their seeds have been ready to sprout when the forest was cut?

They had formed in a warmer time when the tall forest trees were not present or were young and short. There had been no shading umbrella to keep out the pin cherry's needed sun and warmth. The researchers watched. A past cycle repeated itself. A new reservoir of seeds was made as the pin cherry grew taller and denser. The pin cherry itself made the shade the hardwood tree seeds needed to grow. The pin cherry itself was the protective greenhouse for the hardwood plants that grew taller and forced the pin cherry out of the plot. But the pin cherry seeds would wait again for another clear-cut made either by man or by nature.

From Pleasant View's front porch a visitor saw the cut grass lawn, a large, wide weedy field, white birch saplings edging the clearing, and mountains beyond. Visitors might spot a tree encircled by a four-foot-high wire fence —someone's research. Or they might see a strange spongy, yellow foam collar around a telephone pole: The collar was an invention. It collected water that flowed down the pole the way water flowed down the stems and trunks of hardwood trees. When a researcher needed a measurement he often invented a device and technique. Ecologists must devise imaginative equipment.

The botanists knew that transpiring trees give off water and oxygen when they make food. So the trees themselves change the microclimate in the forest—the little climate right around each tree. Air and soil temperatures and moisture are different at different places in the forest. Researchers took the temperature of the air around the top of the canopy and under the tree canopy. They took the temperature of the soils in which the trees were rooted. Differences and changes in the forest microclimates showed in these measurements.

Another biomass measurement taken in the forest was a detritus measurement. Detritus is forest litter. All bits of formerly living things—bud scales, flowers, fruits, leaves, twigs, branches, trunks, logs, and so forth—were collected and measured.

Jim G., doing post-doctoral work at Hubbard Brook, estimated the amount of material falling to make litter, or detritus. He determined the rate of decomposition of the softer materials. As detritus decomposes, its chemicals become available for new plant production and continue to cycle in the ecosystem.

Again, plots were selected at random. Jim cleared his plots of all litter. Then he regularly gathered every new thing that fell in his cleared plot. He set out cloth bags in frames to catch falling leaves. After collecting the detritus, he weighed the litter and converted it to kilograms per hectare. Knowing the amount of detritus for one hectare, he multiplied by the number of hectares in his study plot. Next, he multiplied by the number of hectares in the forest and estimated the detritus standing crop, or biomass, in the study forest ecosystem. Of course he didn't measure only one plot. He measured many plots and took an average of them to estimate the single factor in his multiplication problem.

One of the stranger things visitors saw in the control forest were white plastic funnels. The funnels may have looked like those a cook uses in a kitchen, but their purpose was different. The funnels were taped to three-foot-high sticks stuck in the ground. Jim G. collected the smaller litter, such as flower parts, bud scales, and frass with these funnels.

Frass is hard, tiny round pellets, something like half a BB. Frass is the excrement from the busy munching caterpillars that eat their way through leaf after leaf in the forest.

One of Jim's experiments was to grow caterpillars in a cage. He measured and weighed the frass produced by the leaf-eating caterpillars. Later he collected and weighed the frass collected by his funnels in the field. Knowing the area of the funnel and the area of the study plot, he figured how many funnels would be needed to cover the whole plot. He knew the average amount of frass collected in a funnel. He multiplied the amount of frass in one funnel by the number of funnels needed to cover the whole plot. In the laboratory he counted the number of leaves given to a caterpillar and the amount of frass those leaves produced after the caterpillar had eaten them. Then he could measure frass and estimate how many leaves had been eaten in the forest. He expressed the leaf biomass as kilograms of leaf material per hectare.

The birders measured frass too, but for a different reason. They wanted to discover the number of caterpillars in the forest, the potential bird food. From the amount of frass, they estimated the number of caterpillars needed to make that same amount of frass. As the amount of frass changed, they knew the number of caterpillars changed.

Detritus and frass collecting funnel

Most of the plant studies listed the species present, the plant density, or number of individuals per hectare, and the standing crop, or biomass. Some studies discovered the amount of energy in a standing crop of plants. Biomass was then expressed as calories, or energy, per hectare.

The botanists determined the nutrient, or chemical, content of the plants and their dynamics—the ways the plants affected the environment and the ways the environment affected the plants. The amounts of materials and how they moved or cycled within the ecosystem (intrasystem cycling) were studied too. The plant ecologists learned how materials came into the ecosystem and moved out of the ecosystem. Streams were an important way of moving materials out of the ecosystem, so they measured the chemical content of the water and weighed the biomass of plants and animals floating out of the system.

The researchers studied in order to predict what might happen to the forest and the rivers when changes were made in their ecosystem and the larger ecosystem, Planet Earth. Hubbard Brook research station and more like it around the world could act like a thermometer and take environmental temperatures. Such an eco-study thermometer might tell us whether Earth is sick or healthy.

7

AQUATIC STUDIES: WATER, WATER, WATER

The real laboratory was on the mountainsides where things happened in the forest "test tubes." But a lot of recording, record-keeping, and glass test-tube testing had to be done where it was warm and dry, inside Pleasant View.

Fancy measuring equipment hummed in the enclosed back porch. Shiny glass tubes, petri dishes, and microscope slides glistened. A bunsen burner burned a bright-orange flame that boiled water. The water changed into water vapor, wound through circles of plastic tubing, condensed, and dripped into a glass bottle—distilled. Distilled water was needed for experiments.

Penny, one of Dr. Likens' students, sat in front of two tall glass tubes. Her waist-long honey-colored hair was tied back in a ponytail. Dressed in blue jeans and a loose, wrinkled, faded blue cotton shirt, she hunched over a ledger recording columns of numbers. There was just enough room to walk behind her and watch.

She was titrating water from Mirror Lake. Two long glass tubes hung down from a tall T-shaped holder. Beakers of muddy water caught drips of water from the pointed tip of one tube. Penny turned a screw near the pointed tip. One by one drips of clear liquid fell into the muddy water. Nothing happened. At last one drip seemed to change the color of the water in the beaker from light brown to clear. A few drops of clear water couldn't possibly make that brown water so clean and clear. But the drops were a chemical, not plain water. And it wasn't ordinary muddy water. This water was part of the water samples taken from Mirror Lake. Trying to discover

Glassware used in a filtering system for chemical studies

the amount of oxygen produced by the lake's microscopic green plants, or phytoplankton, Penny had put chemicals in the lake samples when she had collected them. The chemicals turned the samples brown. Indoors she counted and recorded the number of drips of another chemical from the glass tube. This chemical made the water clear again. The number of drips needed to make the brown water clear told her how much oxygen was in her water sample.

Penny had been a chemistry major during her first four years of college. Now, for her master's degree, she was majoring in ecology at Cornell University.

Although Penny's job didn't look very exciting, Penny knew what she was doing and why she was doing it. She rather liked working by herself and making neat pages of numbers. Even if she didn't get to use the data herself, someone else could use her data. Her work might help someone understand our world better.

In the future, if a scientist wanted to know whether the oxygen produced in the lake was increasing or decreasing, he couldn't tell unless he had earlier records, a base line, to compare to his data. A researcher could do the same thing Penny had done and then compare his results with hers and discover what had happened to the lake. Most of the researchers at Pleasant View had to do some tedious and monotonous things—plain old hard work. Penny straightened her shoulders, tossed her ponytail onto her back, and sighed, relaxing.

Research isn't always the excitement that television and movies squeeze into an hour. Of course it has thrilling moments, but those usually come after years of routine and lots of trial and error. New methods, techniques, and experiments for gathering data are tried, repeated, or eliminated. You usually hear only about the successes. But you must be comfortable with trials and errors too. If you discourage easily, you won't like research.

Dave G.'s setup in the basement was a laboratory that looked like something from a Frankenstein show. Frequently Dave disappeared down the stairs under the floor in the dining room. A section of floor could be raised with a large ring. Hinges squeaked. Down the dark, cool stairwell steps led to the old basement with walls of carefully fitted stones. A modernized furnace stood along one wall. A third of the basement shone with an eerie light. Large heavy plastic sheets created a wall around test tubes and large beakers of bubbling water. This improvised lab was the source of the light.

Dave busily recorded data. His experiments had to be kept at 70 degrees. It often got colder than that in New Hampshire, even in the summer. The constant lights took the place of sunlight. In this lab, water from nearby Mirror Lake was tested. Dave added different chemicals to lake samples to see in which water the phytoplankton grew best. He did the same thing with different columns of water in the lake itself, his outdoor laboratory. He added one chemical to one column of water, a second chemical to a second column, a third chemical to a third column, and so on, then periodically checked plant growth in each column. The indoor lab work was a duplication of his outdoor lake work. In this way he checked his lake water figures with a closely controlled experimental situation.

Phytoplankton was the main food source for the primary consumer animals in the lake. It was the beginning of a long food chain for many, many animals, terrestrial as well as aquatic. This tiny little plant indirectly nourished fish-eating bears and humans too.

Having climbed out of the cellar, Dave might close the trapdoor behind him, and walk silently through the back dining room so as not to interrupt the counting of zooplankton, the microscopic animals that live in the lake and feed on phytoplankton. These are primary consumers that became prey for secondary consumers farther along the lake's food chain. Joe, a graduate student of Dr. Likens, spent many hours with his eye glued to a powerful compound microscope that made everything look a hundred times larger. He counted the number of zooplankton in each drop of water on his slide. He counted slide after slide of zooplankton from a fixed amount of lake water. With the help of a mathematical formula that allowed for error, he determined about how many of the tiny little animals were in the lake. If he lost count or was interrupted before he finished a slide, he had to start all over again.

Of these tiny animals that ate plants and floated in the water, over 120 had been identified. The phytoplankton and zooplankton studies were important because these plants and animals were the basic food for the crayfish and the fish in the lake.

In the wintertime Joe made special trips to get lake water and zooplankton samples. He cut a circle in the ice and took his sample from the water beneath. Back at Pleasant View the warmth from the kitchen trash burner always felt very good after such a cold outing.

Joe would not look up as Dave walked down the hall to the front door and joined Dr. Likens and Penny on the porch.

Penny was putting black tape around pint bottles. Every inch of glass was being covered by black tape. Dr. Likens helped her.

The dark bottles helped Penny discover the amount of oxygen the phytoplankton produced. Light passed through the clear glass bottles into the water, but light couldn't get into the dark bottles. Photosynthesis, which needs light, gives off oxygen. In the dark bottles without light, there could be no photosynthesis and no oxygen by-product.

Plants and animals use oxygen to break down their food in a process

Dave Gerhardt's basement laboratory

Phytoplankton

called respiration. Plants not only release oxygen, they use some of what they release.

Penny tried to find out how much oxygen was left over and added to the lake after plants used what they needed. The amount of oxygen was the same in each bottle at the start and the plants in each bottle used the same amount of oxygen. The only difference between the bottles would be the oxygen released by the plants in the clear bottle.

Penny measured the oxygen in both bottles by a chemical method she used in the lab. She subtracted the black-bottle measurement (B) from the clear-bottle measurement (C): $C - B = O_2$, or oxygen added to the lake. The more samples she took, the more numbers she had to average, and the closer her guess came to the real amount of oxygen the phytoplankton added to the lake.

Placing each bottle in its own section of a divided box, Penny moved her empty clear and dark bottles to the back seat of her small bug of a car. Then she roared down the lane to the Mirror Lake road. She made many trips at regular intervals day and night to place new bottles in the lake and bring back stoppered bottles for oxygen counts. In the quiet of the night and early-morning hours light sleepers heard her car and knew Penny was conscientiously doing her job.

One day Penny's Volkswagen had just dipped below the rise in the drive when Dave G. pulled a strange-looking monster from the garage.

Out on the lawn in front of the house Dave shook out three circular rings, like hoops in an old-fashioned skirt. A satiny nylon fabric covered the hoops, joining them together in one long cylinder. Sheryl offered to help hold one end up and looked through the wide tunnel to see Dave at the other end about nine feet away.

Dave floated these "tunnels" in the lake. Open at the top and bottom, they enclosed a column of water in the lake. In them Dave tested his chemical additions to the lake. They kept the rest of the lake water separate from the experimental water columns. He could measure what happened in each column.

You couldn't find such an item in any catalog. Dave had to invent the tunnels or columns to do a job that needed doing. Scientists have to be creative, and these monsters looked like something that belonged in Disney World rather than a science laboratory.

A new carryall truck pulled in next to all the other cars in front of the garage. Dr. Likens met the new visitors, who then gathered the porch chairs around a red table and sat down to wait. Introductions were made. Dr. Margaret Davis from the University of Michigan (now at Yale) had brought her coring team to sample the muddy soils of Mirror Lake's bottom. Dr. Clyde Goulden from the Academy of Natural Sciences in Philadelphia accompanied the group. He was interested in learning what crustaceans, such as the water flea, had lived at Mirror Lake in the recent and distant past. Dr. Davis offered him all the slices of core he would need to do his studies.

Dr. Likens, Dr. Davis, Dr. Goulden, the coring team, and interested students waited patiently for the drilling specialists that Dr. Likens had hired for Dr. Davis. These specialized drillers were the only commercial group that took scientific cores. A sturdy raft was provided for the corers' heavy motor, pipes, and rigging. The corers' truck, loaded with all the necessary equipment, had broken down. A new truck made its way from Pennsylvania to Mirror Lake while everyone waited.

Dr. Likens had extended to Dr. Davis the invitation to core the lake. She seemed calm, as if this type of inconvenience wasn't new to her. The group agreed that samples of earth from below the bottom of the lake were worth waiting for. Though they all sat calmly chitchatting about experiences on other lakes and the work at the Brook, their suppressed excitement and anticipation charged the air with a new vitality. They were eager to get to work.

Dr. Davis was a paleobotanist, a specialist in identifying pollens from past ages. For centuries pollen from trees and plants had been floating onto the lake, sinking, and being covered by silt, dead plants and animals, and the other debris that fill in a lake bottom. Layers of sediments built up, with the oldest at the bottom and the most recent on the top. When hollow pipes were pushed down through these layers of sediments, they would fill with mud in the same order the sediments were laid down in the lake. The long round tube of dirt inside the pipe would be the core that excited the paleobotanists who studied fossil plants. An apple corer retrieves the core of an apple in a similar way.

Specks of dust—ancient pollens—would tell the trained paleobotanist many things. Pollen grains are like pages from nature's history book, telling what happened in the past. The amount and kinds of pollen would tell Dr. Davis what plants had grown in the area during past ages. The rainfall, temperature, and other weather conditions needed to grow those plants were known. Once the plants and climate were known, the zoologist, who studied animals, and the entomologist, who studied insects, could deduce what animals had lived in the area long ago.

Next a geologist would look at the rocks, mountains, and valleys and describe present and past landforms. Like a puzzle, a picture of the past would be created from pieces of evidence, bits of fact found in the present.

The thick, round-looking chocolate cookies in plastic bags stored in Pleasant View's deep freezer were really slices of dirt, samples from other cores. The sections of a core were dated. Scientists knew how many years it took for an inch of sediment to form. They sliced off a piece of years and

Black and clear bottles

froze it until they were ready to put it on slides under a microscope to study.

The crew's excitement was understandable. Had the Hubbard Brook watershed always been a broad-leaved hardwood forest? Had it been a lot colder or warmer or drier or rainier here? Had there ever been glaciers or forests of needled trees like pines or firs? Was the climate gradually changing? Was there a climate pattern? Would a climate period from the past be repeated? They waited with excited suspense eager to find the answers to their questions. Hidden under the Mirror's waters the answers waited.

While they waited, Penny went out on the lake in her boat. Floating orange balls marked her bottle line. Black and clear bottles were attached at different spots to a long rope that she pulled aboard. Last up was the weight that held the line in place. Penny added some chemicals to each bottle. The clear water turned brown, just like the color in the laboratory samples before Penny added other drops of chemicals that turned the brown water clear.

Penny stoppered her two dozen bottles and put each into its own section of a big divided box. She took her samples back to the lab and returned just in time to help row the coring raft into position.

Across the lake floated red-and-white markers that were attached to Dave's monster cylinders. Dave would find his cylinders easily, collect his water samples, and take them back to his basement lab for analysis.

Suddenly a car appeared and backed a large motorboat into the water. Launched, the boat looked like Gulliver in Lilliput as it started circling the small lake. Waves began hitting a small one-man sailboat, a diving raft, and the swimmers. Then even more unbelievably, the boat backed into shallow water, and the driver's son grabbed a towrope and began water-skiing. The trees trapped the roaring reverberation of the engine and the waves grew choppier and choppier. The lake was just too small for so much power. With easier access, plus increasing populations that wish to use small lakes, there may have to be regulations.

Luckily the speedboat gave up just before the research crew came. A big truck took a position on shore ten minutes later. The coring and drilling crew was ready to go to work. They must tunnel back into time before dark.

The raft and pipes were very heavy. Everyone worked together lifting them down and floating them. Loaded with pipes, drill, motor, and winch, the raft was roped to three rowboats. Penny, Dave G., and Jim started rowing out to the center of the lake near the north end. Dr. Likens, Dr. Davis, and Dr. Goulden spelled them at the oars. It wasn't easy work pulling the heavy raft. Finally in position, it was anchored securely. The coring crew took over. The three men who had brought the raft and equipment set up a derrick that looked like the rigging of a miniature oil well. They placed the rig over a hole in the middle of the raft. Next a big, heavy chain that had been wound around an empty oil drum was pulled through the top of the derrick and hooked to the first section of pipe. A spiral drill was attached to the bottom of the pipe. The brake was released and the chain rolled off the drum as thread unwinds from a spool, lowering the drill and pipe into the water. A vise held the first pipe in the raft's round hole while the chain was unhooked and attached to a second pipe, which was pulled into position above the first pipe. A driller fitted the second pipe to the first and lowered them both into the lake. And so it went—one section of pipe was fitted to another and lowered into the water.

When the drill hit bottom, the hard work began. The pipes didn't just slide down as they had. They had to be pushed with all the force the crew could muster into the sediment at the bottom of the lake. Section after section of pipe was pushed through the hole as the drill bore deeper into the sediments, pushing the mud higher into the pipes.

With the last pipe in place, the men paused and rested, hot and tired. Then slowly, carefully, they let the motor wind the chain and pull up the pipes. Section after section was raised, unscrewed, and laid across the raft.

Through the whole operation the scientists again waited. But this time a suppressed joy kept spilling out in jokes and laughter while they rested in the rowboats, feet propped up executive-style.

As the last pipe came up, all the watchers and drilling and coring crews exploded with happy excitement. Even though the oldest, very bottom piece of mud had fallen out, leaving that piece of history hidden, the rest of the cores were good and would keep Dr. Davis busy peering into her microscope for five years. Gradually she would piece her parts of the ecosystem puzzle together and help Dr. Likens reconstruct the area's natural history.

Near shore a girl was sudsing her hair in the lake. On shore, a family cleaned up after dinner. They dumped their hot coals into the lake and left them there. It had not occurred to them to put their cool coals into the trash can. The lake had many different uses and meanings to many different people.

As the coring observers drove back to Pleasant View, they passed the new highway that sent dust into the lake. A narrow corridor of trees between the lake and the highway had been left to preserve a total woods appearance. Would such a corridor of trees between the lake and the highway preserve the lake?

The lake's longevity depended on many things. The normal life of a lake can be anywhere from several thousand to a hundred thousand years, depending on where it is and how it is used. Heavily used and badly treated, a little lake like this in New Hampshire could die in fifty to eighty years.

The corridor of trees might help protect the lake. But sometimes a corridor itself dies because the individual trees need the protection of the larger forest from hot sun, winds, insect borers, plant diseases, or rain runoff. Just because a corridor looks like a forest, doesn't mean it can act like one. That is why there is experimental cutting—to find out whether a good idea for solving conflicts of interests is really workable.

The highway dust might add more silt to the lake, cutting down its algae productivity. The silt could clog up the breathing apparatus of small animals. Dwellings and use could add more fertilizer, greatly increasing the algae productivity. People do not realize their own great power to affect ecosystems. A seemingly permanent, free piece of nature can be easily destroyed.

As the sun set, a starry, dark-blue curtain closed quietly on the day. More acts would follow as scenes unfolded each day at Mirror Lake: swimmers, rowboats and paddle boats, one-person sailboats, children diving from the rocks, a raft blowing back and forth across the lake, picnickers, thin teenagers teasing and being chased, babies in playpens, sunning mothers, workmen eating lunch, and researchers gathering data. All would play important roles in the Mirror Lake drama. Mirror Lake would reflect more than faces through the years—it would reflect the care and concern of the people who used it.

The morning after the coring, a medieval scene of dissection took place in Pleasant View's hallway. On the fifth stair stood the surgeon, Dr. Davis, a scalpel in her plastic-gloved hands. Carefully she cut through a measured muddy glob from the pipe that held a section of sediments from Mirror Lake. In his gloved hand, an assistant held a numbered aluminum pan beneath the glob. The mud slice fell into the pan. He stepped into the dining room, where one of the men waited with his plastic gloves to place the specimen on a glass-enclosed scale. The balance scale measured the wet weight of the specimen to a hundredth of a gram. After drying, the samples would be weighed again, then frozen to preserve them for future study.

Just as you push a stick to get ice cream from a paper cylinder, the coring team used a broomstick and a rubber stopper to push the mud out the top of its tube. Soon the dining table was filled with individual aluminum pie pans each holding a numbered specimen of mud. Five people operated on the cores. As one helper commented, "This isn't the most interesting work I've ever done," but they all knew it was necessary work.

The group of paleobotanists climbed into their rig with cores not only from Mirror Lake, but from other lakes in the area. They had sampled near the shore and from their own boat and raft with their own smaller equipment. The studies and results of these corings would be reported at scientific meetings and written in scientific journals to become part of general scientific knowledge.

8

FISHING, FISHING, FISHING

Dave M., a biology student, did a lot of his fieldwork during the early evening and morning when the fish were biting. He caught 90 percent of his specimens by angling—fishing, fishing, fishing! Two net and six cylindrical wire mesh traps worked for him during the day. He checked these regularly for the small fish.

Midday often found his eye glued to a microscope in the lab next to Penny. He sorted the contents of fish stomachs for clues to fish diets.

One day, Dave took a pickerel from a large bottle filled with formaldehyde, a preserving fluid. He picked up his surgical scissors and expertly snipped the belly of the fish—the medial ventral line, he called it. He laid to each side the flaps of the belly and removed the stomach. Carefully he tied the stomach ends with string to keep the contents from spilling. The stomach was labeled and preserved in a second bottle. During the winter Dave examined stomach contents under a microscope in his college lab.

At Hubbard Brook he worked on one stomach to get a preview of what the food chain in the lake might be. Hard, chitinous (shell-like) parts of a small crayfish were visibly outlined through the milky-colored stomach sac. He opened the gullet with his long tweezers. The scales and bones inside were clues to the food of this one fish.

Some of Dave's lake fish at some time in their small youth had eaten zooplankton like those that busied Joe, who was counting in the dining room. One of his fish, a smallmouth bass, ate abundant terrestrial items like the *Heterocampa* caterpillar Dot was studying.

Dave became interested in watching fish when he was a very young boy

Mirror Lake: Scene of ichthyologist's study

in grade school. At home in his basement he had tank after tank of fish. He just never outgrew his early hobby. And he really did like to fish!

Everyone told Dave that it must be nice to be paid for fishing. But Dave discovered when you *have* to fish, even fishing becomes work at times. On the whole, he believed himself happier doing something he liked in the outdoors. No one can expect 100 percent contentment, and neither did Dave.

The U.S. Fish and Wildlife Service had been Dave's employer when he had worked summers as an assistant for the survey crew of a fish commission. Now his interest in ichthyology—study of fish—had put him on the path to becoming an ichthyologist and a science teacher.

Dave was a quiet person, not given to loud outbursts or long discussions. He was a peaceful person with a strong sense of justice and didn't argue for the sake of argument. He knew the goals for his project and was able to state them clearly and briefly.

First he hoped to find out which species of fish lived in the lake and their approximate numbers. Second, he wanted to determine the most important food for each species. And third, he wanted to see how important a fish was to the life of its predator and how much it fed on other species of fish. For instance, maybe the pickerel ate only crayfish. This fact would make the pickerel a big predator on the crayfish. If it was a big predator and you removed all the pickerel, you might hypothesize or deduce that an increase in the numbers of crayfish would occur. This might be bad or good for the lake, depending upon what you valued or wanted for the lake. If a fish was only an occasional predator of the crayfish, you could hypothesize that there wouldn't be too much change in the crayfish population. So what and how much an animal eats is important in figuring out the future of a given lake or place. Scientists must know what is happening to a lake before they can determine what may happen if they do something different to the lake ecosystem.

After Dave learned what happened in the daily life and seasonal life of the fish, he wanted to investigate the "energetics" of the food chains and food webs in the lake. Since fish are thought of as mobile, changing accumulations of energy and nutrients, Dave wanted to discover how many food calories crustaceans, like crayfish and Joe's zooplankton, and the smaller fish consumed. He also wanted to know how much energy these same fish, the crustaceans and smaller fish, provided for their predators.

Energetic studies of the lake and forest ecosystems were concerned with potential food energy. Food energy was measured by a unit called a calorie—the same kind of calorie dieters count.

A calorie is the amount of heat needed to raise the temperature of 1 gram of water 1 degree centigrade. Four thousand calories is equivalent to about

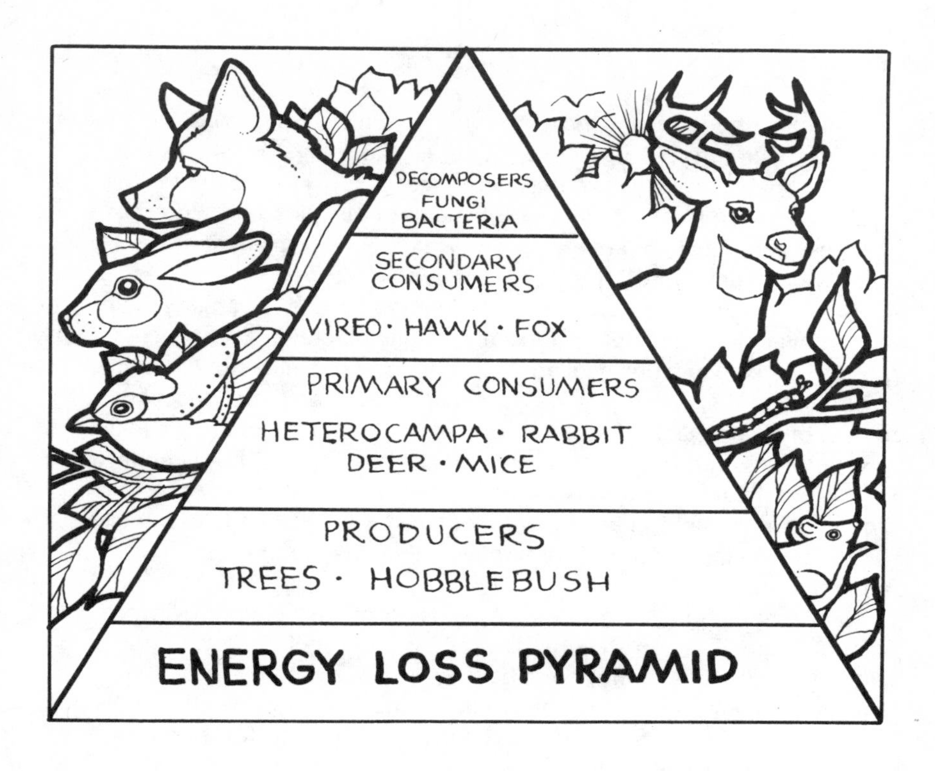

one pound of fat. Energy is transferred from one organism to another by way of their nutrient and consumer relationship, or "who eats whom."

The principle that energy is not made or lost, only changed, may be true. But in an ecosystem, energy can be lost for use in that ecosystem by changing to heat and escaping into the air. When the earth is considered as a single ecosystem, energy can be lost to the atmosphere and space, although some heat may accumulate in space and affect earth.

Energy is lost at each link in a food chain. Some energy is not passed on to the next consumer. A pyramid is often used to show ecosystem energy loss. The number of calories in grass eaten by a cow is more than the number of calories a person receives in eating a cow that ate the grass. Mankind gets more of the sun's energy, or calories, by eating the same weight of plants than by eating animals. A primary consumer, or plant eater, receives more calories from a measured amount of grain than a secondary consumer, or animal eater, who eats meat made from that same amount of grain.

The story about the cat that ate the mouse that ate the malt that lived in the house that Jack built is a food chain story. Energy is lost between each step in a food chain. Energy was lost when the malt was eaten by the mouse and when the mouse was eaten by the cat.

"Lost" energy was energy used by the organism, plant, or animal, to move, make body repairs, grow, reproduce, and, in mammals, to maintain body temperature. To be active, doing all the things organisms do, takes energy. You become aware that body heat is lost in space when you put on a coat or cover yourself with a blanket or sleeping bag. You trap your own escaping heat, or energy, and it warms you. A blanket doesn't bring heat with it, unless, of course, it's an electric blanket.

Nutrients can cycle from one form of life to another, changing their form according to the individual organism's genetic blueprint. Eventually decomposers break up and decay dead organisms. The chemicals of the organisms return to the soil, water, or air as raw materials. Then the chemical building blocks of each organism—the carbon, oxygen, hydrogen, nitrogen, calcium, phosphorous, and other elements are ready to recycle. These chemicals in their solid, liquid, or gaseous forms are part of a system. Even the minerals and gases not used as parts of living organisms are still parts of the ecosystem. Ecosystems contain all the nonliving as well as the living parts of an environment.

While nutrients can cycle in an ecosystem, the energy from the sun cannot cycle. The sun's energy is used and then gone. Such energy is on a one-way street. It cannot cycle back to where it started. The calories Tink and Patsy measured when they burned their twigs showed how much potential energy existed in the wood. But after the wood was burned—using the energy and providing the measurement—that energy could no longer be used in Earth's ecosystem.

You can sketch a diagram on notebook paper showing nutrient cycling with a circle of arrows. Now show energy flow with a straight line of arrows, ending in "heat." Between each arrow on the straight line some heat is lost. Put a zigzag line between each pair of arrows to show this heat loss. Now you can picture for yourself the difference between nutrient cycling and energy flow.

What were the boundaries of Dave's ecosystem study? Where did his ecosystem start and stop?

Like cities, towns, counties, boroughs, megalopolises and "slurbs"—suburbs that go all over the countryside, like Los Angeles County—ecosystems come in all sizes from very tiny or microscopic to the whole earth. The word "system," the way ecologists use it, means a set of things so related or connected as to make a whole. Size just depends on what the ecologist is talking about. Ecologists' systems work. And to work, energy is needed. So every ecosystem has an energy source for its living members, or components. Dave's ecosystem was the lake. Its boundaries were the interface between water and air, and the interface between water and shoreline.

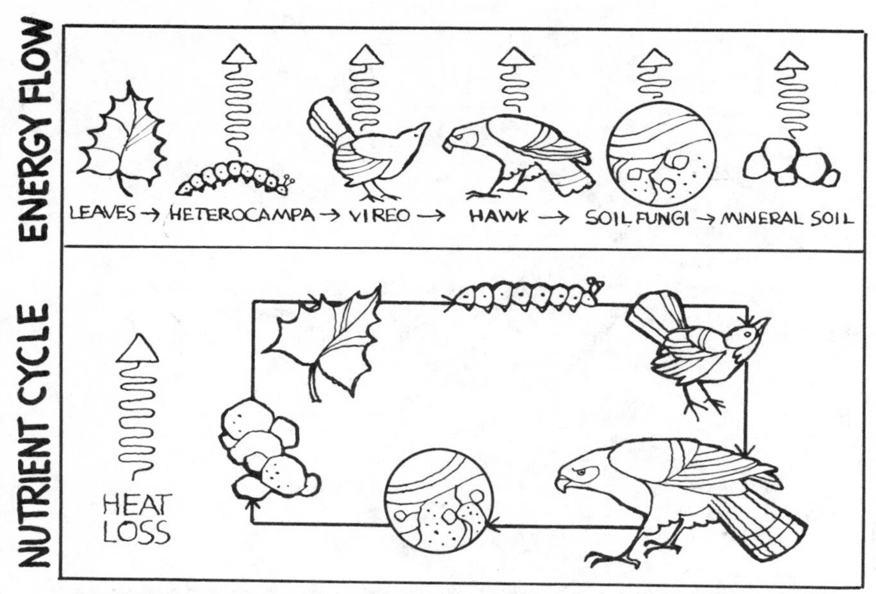

ENERGY LEAVES THE ECOSYSTEM AT EACH POINT IN THE FOOD CHAIN

Ecosystems are open systems. Things come into the lake. Inputs include sunlight, rain, sand, insects, rivers, soap, and so forth. Things go out of the lake. Outputs include water, fish, salamanders, chemicals, and such. But everything in the system affects the whole system in some way. If the something is living, the organism is a part of a community and acts as a link in the ecological chain.

Let's try to synthesize, or put together, our ecosystem information by using the set theory of mathematics. Let a lake, stream, or meadow be an ecosystem, or set. Each ecosystem has many members. Some of the members, or set members, are producers—plants able to trap energy from the sun (energy source for the ecosystem and a set member). The experimental forest, Mirror Lake, Hubbard Brook, or Pleasant View could each be considered separate ecosystems, or sets. And each of these systems, or sets, can be thought of as a subset of the west side of the Hubbard Brook drainage basin, the larger ecosystem, or set. Each drainage basin, including the Hubbard Brook basin, can be considered a subset of the White Mountain range ecosystem.

Next time you eat your lunch, think about ecosystems. You are an ecosystem member, but not a complete ecosystem. You don't have your own energy source. You may have a lot of systems functioning to keep you alive,

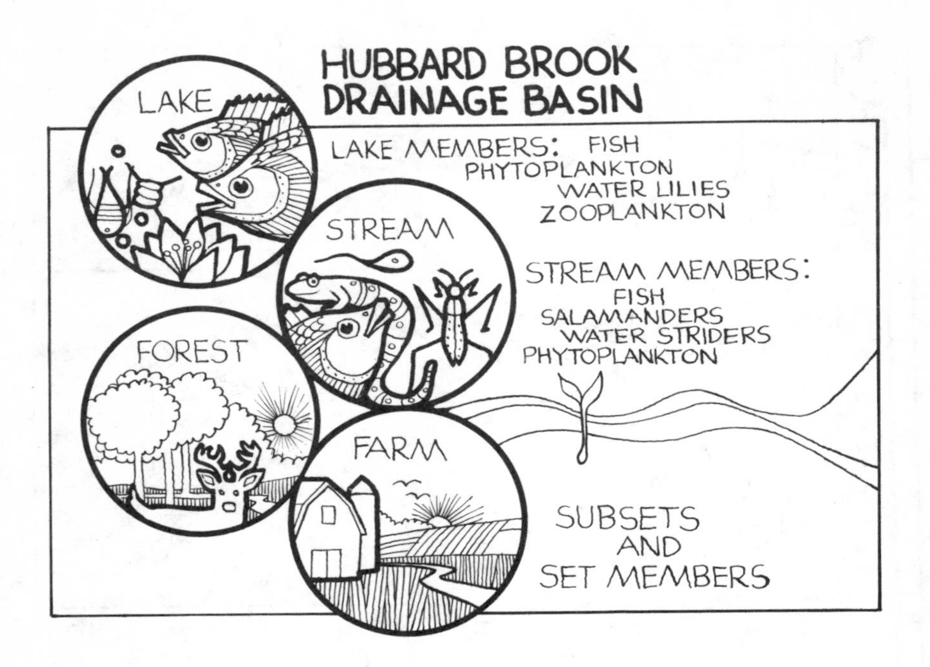

but an ecosystem you are not. You are dependent on a much larger ecosystem—one that includes the farmer's peanuts, grain, cows, and grass, plus all the people and transportation in between that put a peanut butter sandwich and a glass of milk into your hands.

By the end of Dave's Mirror Lake ecosystem study, he had marked and returned 166 fish to the lake and recaptured 39 of them. He had analyzed 132 fish stomachs.

He found five different kinds of fish. He discovered that the diets of the young fish were not the same as the diets of older fish. And he concluded that food might be limiting the growth of the smallmouth bass and the chain pickerel, since the normal adult food items were rare or absent.

Dave found that four elements explained the differences in fish diets: (1) what was available; (2) where the food was in the lake; (3) the size of the predator and its prey—a fish tends to eat something smaller than itself; (4) where the fish had learned to look for food. Fish learned to look for food in certain places. Bass waiting near the surface would be quick to snatch an "input" *Heterocampa* dropping from a tree or flying bird. Perch, which searched elsewhere, would take longer to find an "input" insect.

Dave typed up his findings, passed his oral exam about his thesis, and sent out his job applications. Wherever his job now, Dave can probably be found with a fishing pole in his hand—fishing, fishing, fishing.

9

BIRDS OF A FEATHER

"Birds of a feather flock together," is a saying that applies to ornithologists as well as their subjects. Dick's and Frank's interest in birds began as boys and brought them together to study the birds at Hubbard Brook. These two ornithologists didn't fit the common stereotypes of bird watchers. Dick's six feet eight inches had him ducking under doorways. You would guess his hands handled a football or basketball rather than twenty-gram red-eyed vireos. Frank didn't fit the tennis-shoe bird-watching cartoon version either. Only the binoculars around their necks, the bird guides in their pockets, and their topic of conversation identified them as birders. When they weren't looking directly for a bird, they were always listening. Even in the middle of a "non-bird" conversation a birder noticed a singing whitethroat or catbird.

From birds the interests of the ornithologists had broadened to include ecology. So they had designed a study that would show the interrelationships of birds to their environment.

The ornithology crew's morning started the evening before, when they listened to the weather forecast. Rain meant no netting. Birds trapped and made inactive in a net might die from exposure in a few minutes. Birds lose body heat when they can't move and generate heat by expending energy. When it's very cold, you shake, shiver, and hop around to keep yourself warm. Movement makes your heart beat faster and your blood flow faster, warming you. Or you put on a heavy coat to trap your body heat in the air next to your skin in order to keep warm. A bird's feathers trap its warmed body air just as your coat traps yours. But when rainwater replaces the air next to its skin, a bird loses its body heat rapidly. Wet and immobile in a net, a bird can die from exposure very quickly.

If the weatherman forecasted a clear day, netting and observing on the plot followed.

"Early birds catch the worm," and early "birders" catch the birds. The height of bird activity is before noon. By the time the sun is high and the earth warmed, most birds become less active, awaiting the cooler evening.

Birder alarm clocks rang at five thirty A.M. one typical June day. By six A.M. the crew had finished breakfast, packed their lunches, pulled on their boots, hooked binoculars around their necks, and slipped on long-sleeved shirts or jackets to keep off the early morning chill and biting insects.

Dick warmed up the motor of the green carryall. Frank got in with two bags, each outfitted with color bands, metal Government bands, banding pliers, weighing scales, baby socks, bird guides, and recording books and sheets.

Dot, Dave Z., and Tom S. slid in. Tom and Dave, bird watchers of long standing, were quick and eager to learn anything new, and observed birds as much as they could. Dot's nature interests were more recent, but she was ready to tackle anything on her way to becoming a biologist.

After fifteen minutes and three miles of narrow, curvy, unpaved road, the carryall's steep climb through dense forest and undergrowth stopped abruptly. A wall of forest rose immediately in front of the bumper. Their bird plot was just outside this watershed, number 6.

Dick and Frank had chosen this spot because the conditions were most like Watershed 6, where many plant and waterflow studies were being made. Nearby, the ornithologists could use the results of these studies, while their activities would not interfere with the Watershed 6 study results.

The ornithologists had measured the 10-hectare plot (almost 25 acres) off into 40 squares of about one quarter hectare each. Imagine one-inch squares on graph paper. Now increase the size of the squares to 50 meters (about 165 feet or 55 yards) on each side. At each corner of the quarter-hectare square was a tree wound with a strip of orange plastic tape. A net number was engraved on a metal tag and tied to the orange marker. Near each orange-marked tree and at each corner of the quarter-hectare square, a black net was stretched between two metal poles. Midway between the orange-marked trees, a tree was wound with a yellow plastic strip. The yellow and orange markers guided the researchers to the nets. It was easy to miss seeing a net and to lose oneself in the woods. Up and down weren't dependable guides in this mountain range. You could go down one ridge and up another without meeting a road. The leaves filtered light, making it more difficult to tell time or direction by the sun.

The ornithologists were trying to discover what kinds or species of birds

Unfurling the invisible mist net. Plastic tape marks plot location in forest

were in their plot and how many individuals of each species were present. Like the other researchers, they carried around a whole list of questions in their minds. How many males and females of each species were in the plot? How many nesting pairs were there? In a nesting season, how many broods of young would each pair raise? How many eggs were in a nest? How many of the eggs would hatch and how many birds would fledge? How many broods of young would each pair raise? What was the territory of individual birds and nesting pairs? How large were territories? Which individuals would return to the plots after migration and a nine-month absence? What was the survival rate for each species? What did the birds eat and what predators ate them? Just where were birds linked in the food chain and what was their role—the part they played—in the community life of the forest? After these questions were answered, the ornithologists knew there would be others.

How much of the forest energy rested in the birds? How much of the forest's ecosystem energy did the bird population use? How much of the forest's materials and energy moved into and out of the forest ecosystem through these birds? Did the birds control the insects in the forest or did the number of insects control the number of birds? How did the number of species and quantity of birds found in the cut areas compare to those in the forested area?

Each day's work would bring pieces of the answers to the many questions. Which pieces could never be predicted exactly. How many and which unmarked birds, repeats (birds already banded), or species new to their nets would be caught each day? These were questions that could be answered by midafternoon.

Each day assignments were given out: Dick and Tom would do the census first. Then Tom would do a "wander mapping," while Dick captured birds just outside the plot's boundary for energy experiments.

Dave and Dot would handle C and D lines of nets, while Frank ran the lower A and B lines.

Insect repellant was passed. The odor of the sticky liquid helped ward off black flies, mosquitoes, and no-see-ums that crept into hair and made large welts on the backs of hands and necks—any exposed skin.

Everyone walked rapidly into the cool shade of the forest.

The first thing netters must do is open the nets. Between eight-foot-tall silvery metal poles one inch in diameter a net was wound into a thick black rope. As Dave and Dot unwound the net, a black hammock appeared and then a nearly invisible black badminton-like net stretched taut and covering all the space between the poles to the forest floor.

It certainly would save effort and time not to open the nets each morning and close them before leaving the forest. Leaving them opened all the time would indeed have been easier. But the researchers knew that if a bird can't keep itself warm and fed, it will die. Also, the longer a bird is left in a net the bigger the chance that a chipmunk or another predator might kill it.

A light breeze played with the opened, spidery black web. Its four net pockets stretched forty feet between the poles. When a bird flew between the trees, zap! What seemed to be only a mist of air stopped it and the bird dropped into a web pocket or got caught where it hit. "Mist nets" are well named.

The researchers opened only the number of nets that could be checked in thirty to sixty minutes. On a fair day birds wouldn't die from exposure so quickly. But too many birds trapped in nets at one time would put pressure on the researchers, who practically ran between netting stations and banded rapidly. Time could still be critical.

While Dave and Dot opened their two lines of ten nets, Frank opened his two lines of ten. The lines ran diagonally across the hillside, making the birders hike up and down. Each line was 50 meters above the line below and labeled A, B, C, or D. In each line the nets were numbered 1 to 10. Starting at C-1, Dot and Dave would climb to C-10 then go up 50 meters to D-10, working backward and downward to D-1. Then they would drop down 50 meters to C-1 again, completing a round of the two lines of nets. Frank would do the same with his two lines, A and B. Working at the same time, the ornithologists felt they got a pretty good cross section and coverage of the birds present on the plot.

Dot and Dave worked quickly and smoothly as a team. After all their nets were opened, they kept moving from one net to another, making certain no birds were overlooked because they were partially hidden next to the ground or up in a corner. Leaves or stems that got hooked in the net were removed so that a bird's-eye view saw nothing but empty space between the trees.

Finding birds in the net was like opening presents. As you look forward to a surprise in a package with suspense and excitement, the birders looked forward to surprises in their nets. A new or rare species for this forest, a mother downy woodpecker and her newly fledged brood all filled with downy baby feathers—such finds as these were exciting rewards for the monotonous, hard work.

At C-8 Dot found the first bird. Its beak was sticking through a hole in the net. Wings were entangled, feet ensnarled, and the throat snared by the tiny, almost invisible, nylon threads. The net had done its job well. The bird was almost completely immobile, except for its strong, seed-cracking beak which pinched hard on Dot's finger.

"Ouch," Dot said, letting go of the bird and puzzling over its species.

Dave got out the recording book, pen, and bands as Dot identified her bird.

Extracting a bird from a mist net: least flycatcher ensnarled

Feet are usually freed first

Thread by thread the flycatcher is unsnarled

Weighing a "socked" bird

The bird had the thick beak of the purple finch but it was half again as large. Turning to the plates showing the finch family in Peterson's bird guide, Dot decided the bird was a female rose-breasted grosbeak. The other female grosbeak in the picture, with streaked breast and sides, didn't have so distinct a dark-and-white-stripe pattern across its head. The brilliant rose bib of the male rose-breasted grosbeak gives the species its name.

The delicate job of freeing the bird began. Dot worked the loops of net, now tightly pulled threads, from each claw. She held a freed leg between the second and third fingers of her left hand while her thumb and first finger held the ankle of the other leg. With her right hand she gently pulled thread after thread after thread off each toe. Finally all four toes of the second foot were free too. Grasping both legs gently between her left-hand fingers she pulled the bird away from the netting. But the hooked barbs that join single feathers into one fabric caught the threads and held fast. Patiently, one by one, Dot found each loop and eased it off a feather or over the hard bony elbow and wrist of a wing.

Closing a freed wing against the bird's body, Dot loosened the second wing. When both legs and wings were free, Dot held the small body gently but firmly enclosed in her hand.

The neck and head must be released before the job would be completed. Dave saw that Dot had a problem. While she had pulled the grosbeak away from the net, the tough nylon threads were tightening a noose around its neck. Harder pulling would strangle it.

Dot knew the bird couldn't stay there for long, and other birds might need care in the other nets.

Dave said encouragingly, "There have been times when the job was impossible and we've had to cut a hole in the net. But usually we hadn't been able to get this far."

"Ouch! You stop that!" Dot hollered at the bird.

Taking care to keep her working hand behind bird's head and beak, Dot gently poked a leadless metal pencil under the neck feathers, seeking the tightened threads. Trying one strand and then another, she found a loose loop and pulled it up and over the head and beak. Other threads followed. Finally only one loop remained caught in the bird's mouth. Dot poked the mouth apart with the tip of her pencil.

"Look out, Dot. If you pull the thread straight out it will cut the tongue off!" Dave warned.

The bird's tongue juts up on each side in back. Hooklike pieces of tongue help pull food down its throat. The thread gets caught behind these fleshy barbs. If a birder should pull, the thread would cut the tongue.

"Push the thread backward into her mouth. Back, up, over the top of the tongue and out," Dave suggested.

Free at last. What a relief!

Dave fished a small child's sock from the blue binder that held all the banding and recording materials. He took the bird from Dot, deftly sticking its beak into the sock toe and enclosing the rest of the bird in the tiny sock. Only the tip of its tail was visible. Now the bird wouldn't fuss and could be handled easily.

Dave reached for his notebook and took out a pocket-sized scale that looked like a first-grader's big round green pencil. He clipped a top edge of the sock to the bottom of the scale. The bird dangled while a small marker jumped up and down, finally stopping at 49. "Forty-nine grams," Dot read.

Dave had already recorded the location, date, hour, net number, and weather conditions. Now he entered the bird's weight on the record sheet.

In the bag Dave located his pliers. Especially made for bird banding, the pliers had doughnut-like holes in the middle of the jaws and near the tip. Next, Dave took out silver-colored metal bands. Like wide silver bracelets in various sizes, the bands snuggly ringed very small, small, medium, large, and very large bird legs. Last came colored bands, bracelets made of plastic: red, orange, black, blue, and white.

"Take a number 1A off the wire ring. That should fit this leg," Dave told Dot. "Now read the pressed out numbers on the metal Government band."

Dot squinted to make out the raised numbers.

Dave recorded the number next to the bird's name on the banding sheet. Then he turned to the list of birds for possible color combinations. "Remind me to cross off the colors I use. Otherwise two birds of the same species will be flying around with the same colors and confuse us."

Each color-banded leg marked an individual bird that the birders could identify by sight. Colors easily recognized by the naked eye or through binoculars had been chosen.

"We'll use orange over white." Dave selected from the list of unused color combinations.

Dave removed the scale and placed the grosbeak on his knee. He gently unrolled the upper part of the sock down over the belly, turning the bird so that its right side matched his own right side, its left side matching his own left side.

"This year we're putting the metal bands on the right leg," Dave reminded himself and Dot. He slipped the bracelet around a metal pin on the closed pliers. When he opened the pliers the pin parted, opening the band a little. Then he placed the opened metal band in the pliers' larger round hole and slipped it around the bird's right leg above its ankle. Now he held the leg against the inside of the band so it would clear the spot where the two sides of the band would come together. He squeezed the pliers, closing the silver metal bracelet around the bird's leg.

A female grosbeak gets banded and recorded

Banding kit holds banding tools

Next the bird got an orange band on top of a white band around its left leg. A tiny "shoehorn" slipped these bracelets on easily. Dave crossed off "o/w" under the rose-breasted grosbeak list.

Before setting the grosbeak free, Dave blew up the downy feathers on the bird's lower breast. Dot, looking closely, saw a naked reddish patch under the feathers.

"The brood patch. This female is raising young," Dot reported.

If the sexes of a species have the same color plumage, it can be difficult to determine whether the bird is a male or a female. At this time of year finding a brood patch helped identification.

"Fat O," Dave said, looking at the absence of fat under the bird's skin.

Dot recorded these facts. With all the information noted, Dave rolled the sock over the bird's breast, throat, and beak just as you would roll your own sock off your foot. He clapped his hand over its wings and gently turned it over onto its feet. Resting it on his open palm, Dave took his hand away. In an instant it was gone, flying easily and freely down the hill away from the net.

With his notebook back on his hip, Dave straightened the net, readying it for the next birds. Dot was already sprinting to the next net. She was eager to find what new bird might be waiting for them.

The grosbeak, with her two sets of bracelets, was now part of both the U.S. Government's and the researcher's banding systems. Anyone finding her could read her number, send the number to the U.S. Government, and discover when and where the bird was banded plus other places it might have been captured. The ornithologists had received permits from the Government to capture and band. They reported each bird banded, with its number and other relevant information, to the U.S. Migratory Bird Laboratory at Laurel, Maryland.

This method of tracking birds is the way migration routes and some of the habits of birds have been discovered. The Hubbard Brook researchers always wondered whether anyone in South America would find some of Hubbard Brook's birds. Dave had already been excited and amazed by finding repeats from the previous year's banding. One small vireo had traveled 7,200 miles in nine months—one of nature's regular miracles.

Banding would tell the ornithologists a lot. Dick and Frank and the crew could watch color-banded birds through binoculars and learn how much the birds moved about, what they did, and where their invisible boundary or territory lines were. By watching the plot all year they would learn which birds were permanent residents and which ones were seasonal visitors.

On the morning of our story Frank was having a slow session. He had made his rounds twice, but he had netted only one bird. At A-1 his two daughters joined him. Karen's eyes searched back and forth from the top sections to the lowest pockets of netting. She walked along the net, pulling up the bottom section to better see the pocket near the ground. Midway the net appeared to be caught on a twig. Bending to release the strand, she discovered, instead of a twig, a tiny black-throated blue warbler with its blue-gray back. Its brilliant colors identified it as a male.

Karen pulled open the pocket, putting her right hand over the quiet body. The short, narrow beak stayed closed. The bird lay still. Working carefully, Karen removed strand after strand, freeing legs, body, and head. The netting that had slid smoothly off the body feathers became anchored in primary and secondary wing feathers. Using a fine mechanical pencil, she worked the net over each feather.

As she held wings against body, the net pulled easily off the short head feathers. When she opened the beak, the net fell away completely.

Karen relaxed her hand an instant. The bird took the moment to grab for freedom, flitting out of her grasp and right back into the net.

"Oh, no!" Karen groaned, "We have to do it all over again."

"That happens," Frank said. "Don't get frustrated or discouraged. Just do it again."

This job taught patience. In a short time Karen slid the bird into a sock.

Sheryl opened the permanent-black India-ink pen used for official scientific data recording. Once dry, the ink is waterproof and won't wash away in the rain. Notebook opened on her knees, she recorded as her dad called out the information: "Second bird, June 30, 8:30, A-3, BBW, Male, blue over orange, number 12345–67899, age: AHY (after hatching year)." Hooking the bird on the scale, Frank took off 5 grams for the sock's weight and Sheryl recorded 10 grams. She marked off the blue-over-orange combination on the last sheet.

"Done," Frank said, putting the newly banded warbler into Karen's hand.

She held the bird in her open hand next to the net pole. It waited, not moving. Feeling no restraints, it suddenly darted down and then up to a high limb, paused, and flew out of sight.

Energetically they tramped from one net to the next. Sometimes all three worked to extract birds and "sock" them until their records could be taken. Sometimes the net was empty. After several empty nets and one female scarlet tanager, they came to repeats, two redstarts that had already been banded. Black-hooded with bright red along the leading edge of a wing folded next to a pure white breast, the redstart had large white dots on the underside of its black tail plus outer tail feathers that flicked yellow when the bird was on the move. Appearing at first like a small junco, its quick movements and flashes of red and white gave it away as a redstart.

Frank marveled at the engineering and design that gave these small birds such fantastic flying power. Each bird, only nine grams of flesh, bone, and

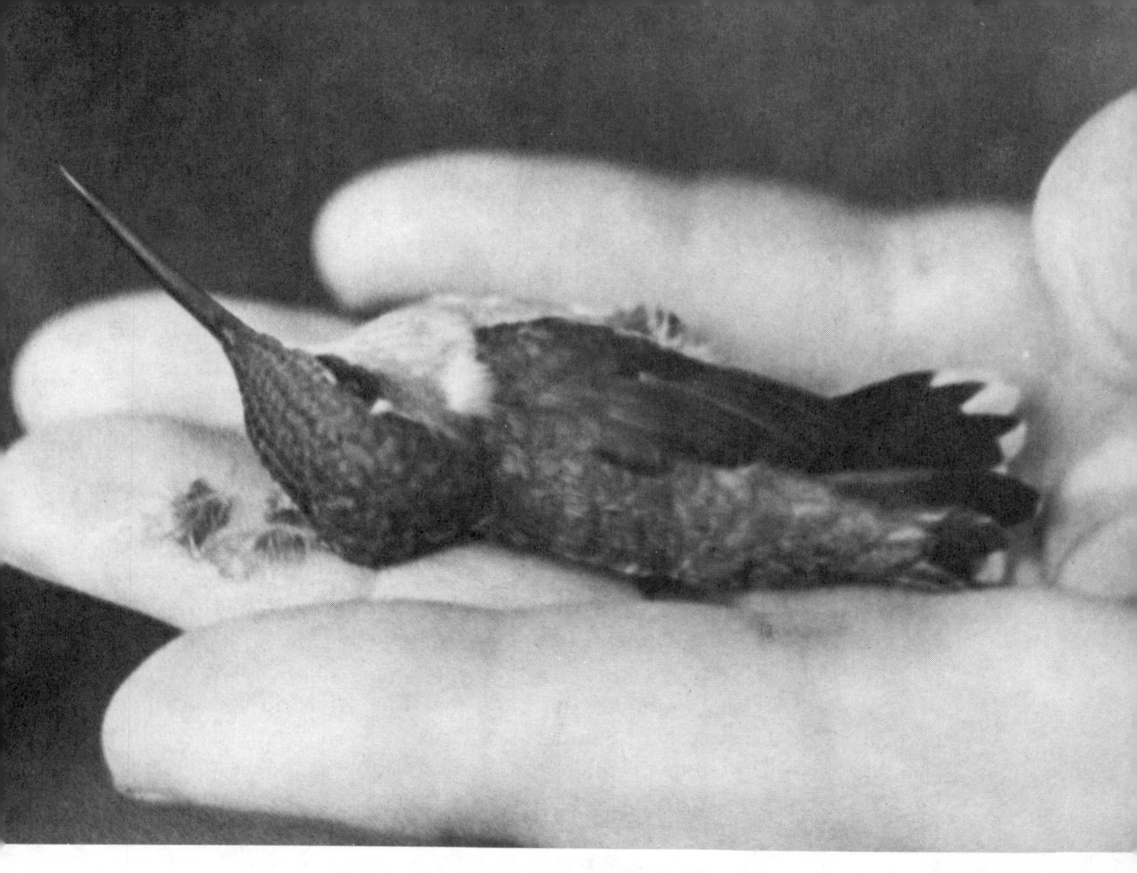

Ruby-throated hummingbird will soon become aware of its freedom and fly away

Flycatcher is gently held by its feet

feathers—no heavier than a letter you'd slip into a mail slot—travels thousands of miles to the Amazon basin in South America. And it comes back again, one round trip every year. How does it make it over those wide spans of water? It can't rest or eat. How can it package enough energy for the trip? How does it store and use its food? Even biochemists don't know the answers. There are still a lot of bird mysteries to be solved.

Sheryl and Karen looked down with respect at the piece of life in their hands. They enjoyed its colors and deeply admired the life force that permitted the redstart its fantastic feats.

Frank was recording each bird in his journal. Over his shoulder Sheryl could make out his cramped inked notes: "6/30/9:30 A.M. A-10. Breeze slight; 5mph from W. Sky: clear, few stratus clouds. Air temp: 70°. Two male redstarts in net. Repeats: Rt.#12345–67879 male, w/r ASY, and Rt.#12345–67849, o/y male, ASY [after second year]. Toward B-9 hear ovenbird, male. Toward A-5 hear wood thrush. Down slope hear vireo."

Closing his journal, he turned to the repeat sheets in the notebook. After recording the numbers, colors, and weights of the two birds beside the date, time, and place, he was ready to go on to the next net.

Why hadn't the girls heard the birds that Frank had just listed in his journal? How did he know he had heard a thrush or an ovenbird? Any bird watcher can tell you that it is not easy to identify songs and calls at first. You have to practice. It helps to have someone point them out to you. Before long you will recognize a few birds. Find a bird singing or giving forth a call note. Then watch and listen at the same time. When next you hear its song or call note, you will remember the song coming from the bird you watched. It is a matter of association. Stop, look, listen!

As Sheryl listened to a calliope of whistles and songs up the slope, Frank pointed out each time two notes repeated themselves. A high note was followed by a note several steps down the scale. "Does tea—cher, tea—cher, tea—cher fit the pattern you're hearing?" he asked.

Listening closely, Sheryl finally fitted the word to the notes. While she listened, Frank pointed to a smallish orange-capped bird in his bird book. Light olive-brown on top, it had a white breast streaked with brown. Its common name was ovenbird, a kind of warbler.

Seiurus aurocapillus is the ovenbird's scientific name. The first name is called its genus—like your surname. The second, *aurocapillus,* is its species name—like your first name. In Latin, *seiurus* means "shake." The ovenbird pumps its tail up and down. The species name, *aurocapillus,* means orange cap and further describes the ovenbird. The bird's nest does look like an old-fashioned earth oven. It is a small rounded dome of leaves and bark on the ground with a doorway the bird can creep into.

Latin is used to name birds as well as plants and other animals, because science tries to be as exact and specific as it can when naming or measuring. These are two of the goals of science: to be exact and to be specific. There might easily be several birds in the world that make nests resembling ovens, or many birds with orange caps. Local people might name a common bird "ovenbird" or "orange cap." But it wouldn't necessarily be the same bird as this ovenbird. If you were visiting and discussed the ovenbird, each person could be talking about a different bird. Information you exchanged about the bird's song, food, behavior, and habitat wouldn't be accurate, because you couldn't be sure you were talking about the very same kind of bird.

Latin has the advantage of being a "dead language." Not used by any people in daily life, it does not change. Words are not getting new meanings or losing old meanings. Fifty years from now a Latin description will mean the same as it does today. An English or French description may not. Since no species of plants or animals have exactly the same Latin names, there are no duplications. When Frank says he saw a *Seiurus aurocapillus,* the same bird appears in every ornithologist's mind.

At B-8 Dave and Dot appeared fifty meters above them. Frank shouted, "How's it going?"

"One sapsucker, one grosbeak, four least flycatchers, two redstarts, and a Swainson's thrush. Pretty low for three hours. What about you?" Dave shouted back.

"A little slow too. One BW, an OB, two RS, a HT and WT and a tanager. Looks like a PF here," Frank answered.

The PF meant purple finch. Between themselves the birders used the initials of the common names for the birds found in this forest. It was a type of oral shorthand. The scientific names in Latin appeared in all their written reports.

Sheryl and Karen were soon at A-2 again. Quickly scanning the net, they pulled the bottom free. Toward the end a chipmunk scampered away from their feet. Looking down, they recognized another redstart, a mass of blood and feathers. Caught low to the ground, the redstart had become prey for a predator, the chipmunk.

Frank took notes, adding "dead" to his records. The other forest animals would reorganize the redstart's materials and energy. Nothing is wasted in a well-balanced forest. But this fact was small comfort to the saddened trio. Researchers always try to minimize the upsetting effect of their own presence or research procedures on the natural community they study. But sometimes their efforts are frustrated, as in the case of the redstart. Without the net, the bird would have escaped this predator.

The rounds went faster as the sun rose overhead. Bird activity had lessened—there were fewer captures. Legs tired, the girls left Frank near noon.

To make the early-morning census, Tom and Dick split the plot in half. Tom walked along B line and Dick walked parallel to him on D line. They could see and hear fifty meters on each side of their lines. Their sightings might overlap on C line, but later they would compare their notes, eliminating from one of their maps the duplicated birds. Proceeding at a rate of six minutes between each net they stopped to listen, observe, and record the species and individuals of birds they saw or heard. They recorded on the map of the plot the approximate location of each song heard and each bird seen.

After completing the morning census, which took an hour, Dick hiked to his net below A line, while Tom continued to wander and map at random the activity he observed and heard anywhere in the plot.

Using binoculars, Tom checked the legs of birds for color bands. He recorded in his journal each bird he saw and its colors, as well as marking the colors and location on his wander map. Tom's work this day would result in more dots on Dave's larger species maps. At the end of the summer a line encircling the sightings would reveal each individual bird's territory.

From April through July male birds establish and maintain territories and sing their identifying songs for the females to hear. The songs are bold declarations of ownership. The "keep out" feeling is strongest toward other birds of the same species.

Even though a bird and his nest takes only a small space in the forest or any other habitat, the bird needs more space—a larger territory—for feeding. A dependable feeding area is necessary to a pair of mated birds raising young. If a bird can keep other birds who compete for the same food out of his territory, he has a better chance of getting enough food for himself and his family. Like a dog, a bird defends his territory.

As Tom walked along that morning, he noticed a bird poised on the outer tip of a twig high above his head. The bird suddenly darted out from its watching post, swooped down to snatch a fly on the wing, and circled back to its branch.

Tom knew that flycatchers don't mind nuthatches, woodpeckers, or sapsuckers who use their specially shaped beaks for getting insects from under the outer bark of trees. The seed eaters, with conical beaks, that stay on the low shrubs and ground don't bother a flycatcher either. But this flycatcher had driven all the other fly-catching birds out of his private feeding ground. Even though no one could see a boundary line or fence, the flycatcher knew his lines and would fight to defend them. A fight to the death or until blood was drawn could happen, but usually didn't. The owner of a territory is often the bolder and more aggressive bird.

Puffing up to look larger, spreading and fluttering his wings, the flycatcher dove toward another flycatcher who had stopped below him on his tree.

Making his beak into a spear, the "owner" of the tree started dive-bombing the invader, while snapping his beak loudly. The intruder flew off, discouraged. He would find a territory with no resident flycatcher.

The closer the time to nesting, the more pugnacious a bird becomes. Once nesting begins, any bird or animal might be attacked if it ventures too close to a nest. Birds will use clever ruses to attract predators away from their nests. Adult birds can be very tricky. Have you ever been led down a hillside by a bird with a broken wing, only to have the bird fly off, leaving you to watch it disappear over the hill?

Tom peered into the hobblebush under an orange tag on a nearby tree. A small, narrow, shallow nest was attached loosely to the stems of the vine. Filling the space were white eggs speckled brown. Dave had found and tagged this nest after he had seen the mother bird fly out of it. If the eggs hatched, the nest would be observed and the number of feeding trips counted. If the researchers were lucky enough to band the birds, the crew could discover whether the fledglings returned to the plot of their birth after migrating.

Nestled in a branching V, shredded birch bark loosely formed a nest that held eggs in a smooth cup at its center. In thirteen or fourteen days, the incubation period, young, naked, blind hatchlings would cry dependently for food.

Tom S. pushed the record button on his tape recorder. "West plot, 2:15 P.M., June 30. Red-eyed vireo nest in D-10. Female sitting; male on branch. Male: step, step, rest. Hop, hop, hop 12 inches, rest; three hops 18 inches. Male flies 15 feet to branch. Rest. Flies thirty feet horizontal; flies ten feet down slope; turns, rest, 3 hops 12 inches. Male flies directly to nest. Rest. Flies up 10 feet. Rest. Hop, hop, hop . . ." Tom recorded everything the bird did in minute detail, letting his tape record the time spent at each activity. The female flew off her nest, hovered in the air, grabbed a caterpillar from a leaf, landed, and whacked that caterpillar to death on a branch. All the activity was recorded.

Back at the house, when the tapes were transcribed, the time involved in all the various activities would be tallied. The energy required for each of the activities could be calculated. Then an estimate of the energy used by the birds on an annual basis could be made and compared to the total light energy captured by forest plants, the producers.

Tom met Dick at the carryall. Dick had captured a red-eyed vireo and a black-throated blue warbler. The birds rested quietly in two green net sacks closed by drawstrings.

"We'll see what they'll eat in captivity," Dick said.

The oxygen consumption of live wild birds needed measuring. Not much information has been recorded about the metabolism of wild birds. In a special glass-enclosed cage at the college the energy wild birds use at rest and when they're active could be measured.

The bird banders closed the nets and met Tom and Dick. It was three thirty P.M. when they drove into the driveway of the farm.

After a swim in the cold lake and dinner, the record-keeping began. Dot recorded each capture on a 3" × 5" card kept for each individual bird. The card showed all the places that one bird had been caught. Some bird cards were filling up because some birds got caught a lot.

Dave plotted on his special map for each species the locations of the birds observed during the censusing and wandering. He identified each individual symbolically by species, color bands, sex, time, and activity. Near the end of the summer, territory lines would be plotted for each bird.

Dick and Frank discussed the day's records and tried to figure out how many mated pairs were nest-building.

The crew enjoyed being in the field looking at birds. The nights and rainy days spent bookkeeping seemed more like work. But one of the main differences between bird watchers and research ornithologists is organized and consistent record-keeping. Eventually, the ornithologists would figure out the general picture from the little bits of facts that were gathered each day.

Bedtime arrived all too soon after the 10 P.M. weather report.

Rain was predicted, so the birders could sleep late—until 8 A.M. They would catch up on their record-keeping the next day.

10

WANTED: ENTOMOLOGIST

No-see-ums sneaked into the hair, eyes, and mouths of the investigators, biting. Buzzing black flies and deer flies added large welts to neck, face, and hands. Even with protective spray and long pants and sleeves, no one escaped the insects.

As workers stumbled over a log, beetles and other insects, along with centipedes and millipedes, scampered for a new hiding place. When researchers grabbed a tree trunk to help pull themselves up a trail, green caterpillars squashed under their hands.

Caterpillar frass pattered like raindrops on the leaves. The hard, round, rice-sized pellets were the digestive discharge from the caterpillars, leftovers from the flat green leaves eaten and used as nutrients for caterpillar life needs. Onto hats, into heads of hair and plastic collecting funnels, the frass fell.

During the first years of ornithology investigation a green moth larva with a red saddle-shaped marking on its back seemed to be everywhere. The caterpillars, in different sizes and stages, were constantly munching leaves. The bare tracery of leaf veins was their calling card. Leaves melted away in their busy mouth parts. Always eating and always on the move to more green leafy material, they ate their way through one skin-splitting size to the next.

The birders, watching the foraging activities of the birds, could quickly see that insects were an important food for many of the birds.

As ecologists, the ornithologists were aware that an important part of the terrestrial life in the ecosystem was not being studied. The big ecosystem puzzle would have one large, empty hole. While Dick and Frank looked at birds, Tom Burton studied the "herps" and Gary studied the mammals. But no one studied the insects, especially the busy caterpillars.

An entomologist—an insect specialist—was needed. But none was on the scene or coming. As ecologists, the principal bird investigators had wide backgrounds in terrestrial organisms. Curiosity about what was happening in the insect world prompted them to call on this background and expand their study to include the insects. They would study the insects in relationship to the birds. What insects were available for bird food? How many insects were available? Which insects did the birds eat?

More questions followed: Which insects were most abundant? Was it possible to estimate their numbers? How were they distributed? Did they fly in the open, just around plants, near the forest canopy or the forest floor, and where in between? After the insects and their behavior had been described by answering these questions, new questions would describe their role in the ecosystem.

What did the most abundant insects eat? What was the nutrient content of the insect population? What were the total roles of the insects in nutrient cycling compared to other animal populations? Did the insects move the forest nutrients around a lot or very little?

It would take years to get the answers to all these questions. But when the answers came, the forest study would have more base lines—numbers that could be compared in the future. It would take several years to develop field techniques, or ways of collecting, that would enable reliable data, or numbers, to build up.

Thinking up the methods and procedures to find the answers to the questions was a creative and inventive part of the research. A forest lab is not so easy to manipulate or control as an indoor laboratory. Accurate measurements are harder to get. Weather alone may spoil several days or weeks for data-collecting.

The new entomology team decided their first job was to find out more about the life cycle of the green caterpillar. Their second job was to figure out how to get samples of insects from different heights in the forest. The third job was to find someone who could help identify insects. Their last job was to analyze the data.

Whenever a scientist begins a study, he turns to the reports of others. He reads articles by scientists who have faced similar problems. Reading may give him some ideas for solving his own research problems. What is not known or reported by others, the scientist must discover for himself. Then he will write up his methods and discoveries to share.

The printed reports suggested a population cycle of about ten years for *Heterocampa,* the smooth green caterpillar with brown spots and a red

Caterpillar picking

saddle in some of its stages. The population numbers would increase and then go down until the caterpillar was almost gone. The investigators could observe the caterpillar and see if the same cycle happened in their forest. If it did, they could expect another peak in numbers about 1980.

In order to count *Heterocampa,* the researchers had to be able to recognize it in its different stages, or instars, in the field. So they put one of the student assistants in charge of a caterpillar nursery.

Dot learned about the life history of *Heterocampa*. *Heterocampa* was the genus name for a group of moths. "Saddled prominent" was the type of *Heterocampa* that Dot was trying to raise and observe. She learned to recognize each of its five instars. She discovered how much each instar ate and how much frass each one produced. She found they really liked beech leaves.

Very small *Heterocampa* were put into pint glass canning jars with the leaves they had been eating when they were plucked from a tree. Tree limbs had to be cut and leaves picked to keep them munching.

Small problems popped up. The cotton cheesecloth squares that covered the jars were held in place by wide rubber bands. Small caterpillars crawled up the jars, over the lip, under the cheesecloth, and escaped down the spiral threads at the top of the jar like a hiker winding down a mountain trail. Metal lids were out because Dot was keeping caterpillars, not canning them. They needed air to stay alive!

In the dining room Pat Sturges watched as escaping caterpillars were caught and returned to their jars. She thought awhile and suggested trying the screw rings that usually came with canning jars, but keeping the cheesecloth lids. Dot tried it. Sure enough, the rings twisted the cheesecloth into the glass threads and blocked the escape route of the caterpillars.

Dot observed the growing larvae. She took notes about their size, shape, appearance, and the number of leaves each larva ate each day. As they shed their skins and grew bigger, she had to watch each molt carefully so she would be able to recognize the original larva through all its instars, or stages of caterpillar life. "Look at this one!" she yelled, focusing the binocular microscope. Everyone looked so they could recognize the instars too. Dot described each stage in her notebook to help the other researchers identify them. In the first instar horns appeared on the head. The third instar no longer had horns, but showed a saddle on its back. The fifth instar dropped to the ground and burrowed in the litter as a pupa with a hard covering. The next summer an adult moth would emerge from the pupa.

The saddled prominents made good food for the captive birds awaiting transport to the biology lab at Dartmouth college where respiration studies of them took place.

Birds eat a lot. The supply of live *Heterocampa* was often low. So sometimes Frank and his family went *Heterocampa* picking in the woods outside the experimental forest zones. As if they were blackberry picking, they found each caterpillar, plucked it from its leaf, and put it in a plastic bag. Finding the well-camouflaged green caterpillars was difficult. The caterpillars matched the piece of leaf they were eating. Sharp eyes were needed to spot them. Often, clues were used to locate them—a half-eaten leaf, veins on a half leafless tree. A visitor in the woods might have thought the season was fall rather than summer—so many trees had lost a large part of their leaves.

Frass collection was one way of trying to estimate the number of insects in the forest. Dot recorded the weight of leaves put in each jar and the amount of frass taken from each jar. Soon the researchers could tell how much frass was made by one insect's eating a certain mass of leaves. Using Jim's measurements of frass in the field, they figured the number of leaves eaten and the number of caterpillars needed to eat that number of leaves and make the measured amount of frass: *F*rass weight tells *l*eaf weight tells number of *c*aterpillars *(F→L→C)*.

Another way of estimating the relative number of insects in the forest was to trap them and count them. Stationary traps were put out at special places near the bird grid and checked regularly. The researchers figured out how many insects per day, per week, and so on, were caught.

Several kinds of traps were used to see which ones worked best in this forest. Aerial nets, night-light traps, glass and water traps, malaise net traps, a suction trap, and a poison bag trap were tried.

A stick with an attached cone-shaped net made an aerial net. With this butterfly net a collector made measured sweeps through the air at regular heights a certain number of times a day and week. There are standard ways for using this net. The insects were removed from the net and placed in a killing jar.

The jar contained a poison deadly not only to insects, but to humans too. Plaster of paris was hardened over potassium cyanide, sealing the poison off from the rest of the jar. A blotter covered the plaster of paris. Fumes seeping through killed the insects painlessly in seconds. The collector was very careful not to touch or smell the poison or drop the bottle.

An entomology student told the children at the station that his jar was too dangerous for them to use. After they swept the meadows with their nets to collect their own insects, they used their own killing jars. Ethyl acetate, or fingernail polish remover, was soaked in cotton and stapled to the cardboard liners in the lids of their bottles.

Battery-operated light traps with ultraviolet bulbs were set out in the forest to catch night-flying insects. Placed over a bucket holding poison, the light attracted insects, which were overcome by the fumes and dropped into

Malaise trap: insects inside netting go to top of trap.

Tired, they drop into funnel and killing jar

Suction trap

Batteries, generator, and transformer provide power for suction trap

the bucket. This trap was used one night every two weeks. Researchers only wished to sample what was there, not to kill everything in the trapping area.

The glass and water trap was made of a 1½-foot square of clear rigid plastic. A 3½-foot two-legged frame supported it vertically above the ground. Insects flying through the forest hit the plastic and fell into the water-filled trough under the glass. Detergent in the water wetted the flying insects and caused them to sink and drown. When the board split and leaked, data were lost and researchers were frustrated.

Malaise net traps looked like a net tent with a center pole. Four flaps, or vanes, were held out with rope, making four corners to the "tent." Insects hit the vanes, crawled upward instinctively, climbed into the clear glass at the top center point of the tent, and fell into a funnel that led to a poison jar. Every two days the insects were collected.

Ideas to solve problems might come from any place. The suction trap was an idea that Dick brought back with him from a stay in England. Used there in farming, it now collected forest insects. An electrically run fan created a suction and moved air down through a fine mesh screen cone. Insects in the air near the trap were pulled down with the airstream into a collecting cylinder below. Each hour a round disk fell and separated insects according to the hour they were collected. The cylinder containing the collection of insects was removed once a day. Each layer of insects was put into a separate small envelope and labeled by date, hour, and the height of the trap.

How to plug in an electrically operated suction trap in the woods was a problem with a quick answer—use a gasoline engine to run two automotive alternators that make electricity and send 12-volt charges into a storage battery. An automobile electric light system works in a similar way. But the suction fan needed 110-volt alternating current to run. So, after leaving the batteries, the 12 volts were put through a small square converter box to be changed into the necessary 110-volt alternating current. Then the suction fan could be plugged in. The answer came quickly, but getting everything into the forest and working was another story.

For three frustrating weeks much of the researchers' time was spent trying to make machinery work. Luckily they had the help of a college technician. His job was keeping the college scientific instruments and equipment running and the scientists working. He also devised new equipment to do specialized jobs. He now used some of his own time to visit the woods and work out the kinks in the heavy, cumbersome equipment. Finally, gasoline energy was successfully changed into electrical energy. The fans under the traps hummed quietly. The disks gave a metallic clink hourly as an electric current released a metal lever that held the twenty-four disks in place.

A king-sized sheet of heavy plastic was anchored at four corners to make a protective tent over the machinery. The equipment to keep two traps running took several times the space of the two three-foot traps.

Craig collected insects by putting a poisoned bag over branches of the trees used by the black-throated blue warbler. He shook the contents of a branch into a bag. Later he identified and counted the insects in the bag to learn which ones were possible food for his birds.

All these traps caught insects near the forest floor. But how to sample the canopy of trees fifty to seventy feet tall?

Everyone brainstormed. Suggestions flew. The investigators and their friends said anything that came into their heads while trying to figure out what could work:

Spikes and a safety belt—too dangerous for inexperienced climbers. Broken body parts mend slowly.

Use a cherry picker such as the telephone and electric men use to reach high wires. The farmers used similar mechanical baskets to stand in while picking the tops of their trees. Why not pick insects the same way? No roads. Too difficult to get into the forest without upsetting the outdoor laboratory.

Hire a smart monkey—ridiculous!

What about a high, open tower like the one on Watershed 6? Air temperatures were measured at different elevations—why not measure insects the same way?

And so the suggestions came.

Using the framework open tower seemed the most practical idea. Tower sampling would be supplemented with the help of a professional tree climber. Later Dick would adapt the air sampler even further with ropes swung Tarzan-style to the tops of the trees.

At first, the idea of climbing trees had not appealed to all the researchers —one had experienced a fall. On second thought the idea did seem workable, if they could get an expert to do the climbing. Rod was their man. He was a professional tree trimmer and pole climber. He knew how to use a safety rope to break a fall in case his spikes let him down.

So the entomology researchers hired Rod to climb for them every ten days for eight weeks. Each time, a total of approximately 64,800 leaves (18 trees times 3,600 leaves) were examined for any sign of insects.

At random Frank or Dick picked out representative trees. Rod started the upward climb, moving his hands up the tree trunk as he scampered to the top part. Instead of a smart monkey, they had found a smart man who could climb like a monkey.

Rod had had falls during his career, but he had always gone back to his chosen occupation. He put the researchers' hearts in their throats a couple of times. His spikes slipped, and he made a free fall halfway down the tree before his rope jerked him to a stop.

Up into the treetops by climbing the red tower

Recording thermograph and anemometer on tower record weather variations at different heights

Rod cut twelve limbs at random from the upper, middle, and lower part of each tall tree. Three kinds of trees were sampled and six trees of each kind. One member of the counting team caught branches and distributed them to other team members positioned here and there on the forest floor. Under their breath they all counted. Examining ten leaves, Tom S. called to Patsy, the day's recorder: "Ten [leaves], one [insect], third [instar: stage of development]."

Dave called, right after Tom, "Ten [leaves], one [number of insects], fourth [instar]."

Tom S. followed quickly with "50; 2, third; 1, fourth; and 2 geometrids (inchworm eggs)."

Frank hollered, taking his turn, "60; zip [zero]."

Pat wrote frantically, trying to keep all the numbers straight and under the correct caller's name.

Back at Pleasant View, Frank did the tabulation. He found out how many of each insect were on the 1,200 leaves at each of the three levels in each tree sampled. After sampling eight times and inspecting 172,800 leaves for each kind of tree, the researchers estimated the number of insects they could expect to find on the leaves of an average tree.

An estimate is an educated guess—a guess based on some facts already known. Knowing the number of leaves and the average number of insects per leaf, the researchers could estimate the number of insects in their plots and in the whole experimental forest. By doing the same sampling each year, they could compare each year's results with the first reliable year's samples. The sampling would tell whether the number of insects was increasing, decreasing, or staying the same. The more leaves inspected, the smaller the guessing error and the closer to the real number the scientists would come. Ideally, they would look at all the leaves in the forest on the same day, but that, of course, would be impossible.

Trying to schedule Rod for good-weather days was hard. Weather forecasters had their troubles predicting too. Mostly, the researchers were lucky.

But one morning everyone was working as quickly as possible to finish counting the required number of leaves. Although the sky overhead was sunny, rolling peals of thunder sounded. To the experienced forest worker, that meant a thundershower. As the thunder got louder, a circle of clouds darkened and moved inward, filling the sunny space over the forest. Suddenly the light was turned off. The researchers felt as if they had stepped into a dark closet and the door was closing. Eyes accustomed to the light had not accommodated to the quick change. Someone joked, "Where's your flashlight?"

Rod reached the forest floor as "20; zip" finished the leaf count and peals of thunder brought buckets of rain. Pressing close to the tree trunks, the researchers hoped the leaves and limbs above would act as an umbrella. At first they stayed dry as the floor around them turned wet and slippery. But after ten minutes "umbrellas" began to leak. As they got wetter and wetter, the researchers felt colder and colder. With nothing to lose, they made their way directly back to the truck, trying not to slip and add injury or mud to chilled wetness. The metal notebook was tightly closed. The day's data wouldn't wash away.

Besides a tree climber, the investigators decided to use a steel tower. The ornithology, ecology, and entomology researchers, with the help of their students and summer workers, became tower builders. Leveled on railroad ties, the heavy steel six-foot scaffolding grew like a column of tinker-toys. One open square was attached to another. The weight of each section held the tower in place. But as it grew taller, it swayed. Workers attached strong guy lines to each upper corner of the tower and anchored them near the forest floor. The lines held the tower securely balanced. Now workers would not get seasick as they climbed the tower to watch caterpillar larvae on the leaves in the treetops. Several people chose not to look down, since they suffered from slight cases of acrophobia, or fear of heights. It was a good place to get a suntan, high in the canopy.

Boards placed across the beams at several levels held recording thermometers. Researchers stood on the platforms to count insects. Tower data was compared with and added to limb-cutting data.

Temperature data was included with insect data. Someone might be interested to learn whether temperature affected insect numbers at the altitude where they were found.

The researchers planned to place malaise traps at different levels on the tower and take samples from the forest floor to the treetops. Some insects had limited elevation levels in their life histories. If all elevations were not sampled, some kinds of insects might go undetected.

But plans and methods changed as researchers learned from experience and got new ideas from other people and places. They adapted such ideas to meet their own needs. The suction trap started Dick thinking and inventing. He would have to wait for more malaise traps. The company was out of them. Suction traps were available—he had had two shipped to New Hampshire from England.

Dick figured out another way to sample insects at varying elevations in the forest. The highest tree limbs near the tower were used to hold ropes tied to the traps. Pulleys raised and lowered the traps to any height. Hoisting the traps into the treetops and down to the forest floor worked very well.

One trap remained all day at one level. The next day the same trap collected at a second level and so on through five levels and five days. The second trap changed levels every three hours during the day, with no changes between 8 P.M. and 8 A.M. the following morning. After five days the traps switched jobs and carried out new schedules. Disks fell and collected hourly samples of insects throughout the day, every day. The recording thermometers on the tower traced the temperatures at the five levels on their graph-paper-covered drums. Each hourly collection of insects had the date, level, hour, and temperature recorded on its envelope.

An ornithology student named Craig devised another way of getting up into the middle levels of tall trees—a ladder. His first ladder let him down because the plastic connection from the ladder to the tree was not sturdy enough. Luckily he grabbed a branch that broke his thirty-foot fall. Craig was philosophical about his broken invention: "It now rests with all the other inventive failures on the Hubbard Brook junk heap!" His second ladder was held in place by rigid iron piping. This one worked. He could take his poison bags higher up the tree and sample the insects in the branches. He discovered what insects were on the "cafeteria menu" awaiting selection by his black-throated blue warblers.

Collecting insects and frass, examining bird's stomachs, and counting insects on leaves were all ways to get information about insects.

Litter-sorting a measured area of forest floor was another way to collect insects. Once every two weeks an empty square frame about 20×50 centimeters was sunk into the litter on the forest floor. Everything inside the square was placed in a plastic bag. The bag was tied and the sample dated. Later, on a table in the dining room or on the front porch of Pleasant View, the litter was spread on a tray and sorted by hand. All the insects were removed. Identifying, counting, and preserving samples of each kind of insect followed.

Bird stomachs were also dissected. A microscope was used to identify insect parts. These findings told exactly which insects the birds had eaten.

Frass-collecting was done by placing paper filters in white plastic funnels. Three-foot sticks stuck into the ground held the funnels in place at special spots on the birders' grid map.

Wet paper filters tore easily. Rain added to the difficulty of getting good samples and typical numbers. The frass fell through torn paper funnels. This type of problem existed for all the researchers working in the outdoor lab, where control of all the variable things that can happen was impossible. Samples frequently had to be taken again and again. Days, weeks, months, or years might be added before reliable samples and numbers could be worked into formulas that revealed forest secrets.

All these trapping and collecting methods helped tell how many insects were in the woods, which insects were most plentiful, and which insects were in the birds' food chains.

Frank gives Craig's newest insect sampling ladder a trial

To help solve the researchers' third problem, help in identifying insects, another Tom came to claim a bed at Pleasant View. The staff was fortunate to find an undergraduate student trained in entomology. Tom Baker planned to become an entomologist. He had a good insect background as well as keen interest. He was a careful observer and knew how to follow a key, identifying the insects as to order and family. He also knew how to preserve insects by a standard museum technique, drying specimens on pins. His insect labels were neat and accurate.

Like Joe, Tom needed good eyes. He spent many many hours a day peering into his binocular microscope. He carefully examined insect parts taken from bird stomachs. With his keying manual open beside the binoc, he looked at whole insects, noticing special features that identified them.

Tom not only keyed insects, analyzed bird stomach contents, pinned, and labeled, he also collected specimens. Collecting was a good change in activity from the steady sitting at the binoc.

With his net, Tom swept the air in the forest study areas. Sometimes he swept the air above the fields in front of Pleasant View just for practice and to satisfy his curiosity. He wanted to see what was there and how field insects compared with the forest insects.

His forest sweeps were made one or two times a week at regular times and at special places on the grid system. That is one important thing about data-collecting. The researchers did not collect on whim—whenever they felt like it. They collected regularly in a set manner. This is the only way investigators can accurately compare one day's collecting with another and one year's collecting results with another year's results.

Tom also did litter-sorting. He collected and tried to identify grubs and insect life of all kinds in any stage—larva, pupa, adult. He counted the organisms and sorted out the ones he didn't know. For many, there was no way to get a name. Later he tried to key out as many unknowns as he could. In this way he learned to recognize the insects by sight.

The new entomology team attacked the insect study as tenaciously as the insects attacked the researchers. With hard work, luck, and time, a gap in the eco-puzzle would slowly be pieced together and filled.

Toad is a well-camouflaged amphibian

11

TURNING STONES

Frogs, toads, and salamanders are amphibians. Snakes, lizards, and turtles are reptiles. All are vertebrate or backboned animals and cold-blooded. They do not have a thermostat inside them, as do the warm-blooded mammals and birds. Internal temperatures of warm-blooded animals stay about the same. For humans the temperature is 98.6 degrees. Cold-blooded animals have a much wider range of body temperatures. If the air temperature is very warm, a salamander's temperature rises to match the air temperature. If the air temperature gets very cool, the salamander's temperature becomes low too. Low temperatures make salamanders sluggish. If the temperature gets too cold or freezing, the salamander will freeze to death. Covering itself up would not help. It has little body heat to trap.

Herpetology is the study of the cold-blooded animals—reptiles and amphibians. A herpetologist is the person who does the studying. He nicknames the animals he studies "herps."

A warm-blooded Louisianian became the cold-blooded herpetologist at Hubbard Brook. His trademark was a warm wool plaid jacket. He would wear his jacket when other people were already too warm. He delighted in muggy hot days that caused the other researchers discomfort. A former high school science teacher, Tom Burton followed his own curiosity, background, and interests in picking a topic to study for his Ph.D. research under Dr. Likens.

Which salamanders were in and near the streams and lake? How many of each type were there? Which salamanders were most plentiful? To discover the answers and fit the information into the eco-puzzle were Tom's goals. He also hoped to learn what role salamanders played in the ecosystem action—the nutrient cycling and energy flow.

Tom made some preliminary surveys and found out what kinds of salamanders he could expect to find. Next he did his homework. Forest investigators, like private eyes, have to find their "man." Knowing the habits of salamanders and where they might be found helped. Special books of keys and facts told Tom what was known about the salamanders he found.

He read about courtship patterns, breeding time, where to find salamander eggs, and how long the adults stayed with the eggs and young. He learned how long the salamanders were larvae and whether the adults lived near stream edges, stayed in the water itself, or lived entirely on the land, away from water except to lay their eggs. From his reading, Tom learned the most likely places to find his salamanders. He also learned what facts were missing from the life histories of the five salamanders he discovered in his study plots.

Hoping to learn new facts about salamanders, Tom checked to see whether appearance and behavior of the salamanders he found fitted the book descriptions.

Not much was known about the purple salamander. Population estimates were rare and based on little evidence. Tom wanted to compare his counts with published studies. No counts were known for the two-lined salamander or the purple, or the land stage of the red-spotted newt, although their densities in ponds were recorded as high.

Tom captured, marked, and counted. Knowing the original number of animals he had marked and the number of recaptured animals, marked or unmarked, Tom could use an accepted method for figuring total numbers of organisms just the way Dave M. had figured his numbers and the density of fish in the lake.

Using printed studies of others and his own life-history studies, Tom discovered the microhabitat of his salamanders. He made gut analyses himself to learn the kinds of food his salamanders ate. The food eaten was a good clue to where the salamander lived. The adult salamanders ate land invertebrates. Their prey was as large as they could manage to eat.

The salamander chose its place in the forest, or microhabitat, by moisture and temperature. In spring, summer, and autumn, the Hubbard Brook Forest was just right. But winter cold killed a lot of salamanders. The death rate went up.

Other researchers added to Tom's investigation as they made discoveries. Tom Baker, the entomologist, found the remains of a red-backed salamander in a wood thrush. Other predators of the red-backed salamander were Eastern garter snakes, shrews, ground-foraging birds, and the purple salamanders.

Tom's goals were similar to the goals of other vertebrate researchers who studied fish, birds, and mammals. He could use similar statistical methods, but the ways he captured and marked had to be much different. Salamanders were not like mice, birds, fish, or caterpillars.

Tom's first problem was finding a place to sample. How could he disrupt the forest floor without interfering with the measurements of other studies? The Forest Service solved this problem. Tom sampled W4 before the Forest Service cut it as part of their experimenting.

Sampling thirty plots, each 25 meters square, was quite a job! He turned all the logs and rocks. He opened logs and raked deeply into the litter with his potato rake. It took five hours to cover each sample. He spent from one thousand to fifteen hundred hours sampling on dry days.

Tom found 450 *Gyrinophilus p. porphyriticus,* or purple salamanders, in W4. The purple salamander kept to itself and was hard to find. It was rare. On rainy nights during the warm summer it came out to look for food. The red-backed salamander, *Plethodon c. cinereus,* preferred wet nights to move on top of the rain-soaked litter.

Tom found himself with rainy night work. Gary, a mammalogist, lent Tom a hand and provided company.

Tom and Gary would leave close to the witching hour of midnight. They quietly sneaked out of the house wearing tennis shoes and carrying flashlights. They entered the pitch-black forest in the pouring rain and were soon ankle-deep in the spongy litter. But the salamanders were having a great time. Humans and salamanders do not always enjoy the same microenvironment!

Lines 120 meters long were set out and each line was sampled once on rainy nights. The location for each salamander was recorded. Its position on the plants or litter was noted. In three sample nights 2,055; 2,367; and 885 salamanders per hectare were counted.

After three hours of sampling, two drenched researchers would return to the farmhouse. They put on dry clothes and wrung out their wet ones. They put something hot in their hands and stomachs to quiet their shaking and chills. Besides strong legs to climb mountains, the researchers needed good health in order to recover quickly from exposure.

To figure out the average salamander population in streams, Tom sampled the pools, then totaled the numbers captured in each pool. Next he divided by the number of pools he had sampled. This gave him the average population per pool. Then he multiplied the average population per pool by the total number of pools he had counted in the stream section he had studied. Now he had the approximate total number of salamanders in the study stream.

Of course, the actual number of salamanders in each pool probably varied from the average—just as the average number of children in a classroom in any state may not tell the exact number of students in any one classroom. The average tells about how many. The exact number varies.

Tom figured an allowance for variance by a mathematical formula. Then he could say with a fair amount of certainty the least and most salamanders that he might find in any pool.

Tom used the mark and recapture technique in 22 pools out of the 243 he sampled. He sampled the lower, middle, and upper parts of the stream. He marked the salamanders on their toes. Two weeks later he sampled the same pools where he had marked salamanders and recaptured some. He knew the number marked and the total number recaptured that were previously marked. With a formula he could figure out his population estimates. The population estimates could be translated into biomass per hectare measurements. By using the bomb calorimeter, he measured the calories per hectare in his salamander populations.

Into Tom's field notebook went several measurements when he caught a specimen. Snout-to-vent and total-length measurements were recorded for each salamander. The temperature of the soil and the moisture present were recorded. The limnologists had already figured out the discharge, velocity, temperature, and chemistry of the streams Tom sampled. The cooperation of other researchers and the use of their findings saved Tom time—time he spent on his salamander study. Everyone's individual study benefited in some way from the studies of another researcher.

One clear warm day Pat followed Tom up a stream in W4. She wanted to see what a herpetologist did in the field.

It was a muggy morning at the farm. The heat haze from the water droplets in the air, backlighted by the early sun, made a screen in front of the distant mountains. It felt cooler under the trees and along the stream. Pat appreciated the air conditioning job the forest did.

Tom started turning rocks in the stream. Pat watched him lift a rock, turn it on its side, check for salamanders, and put the rock right back where it had been. A new difficulty in an outdoor lab appeared as they kept a wide eye open for darting salamanders. Fine silt mixed into the water as Tom turned the rocks. The muddying effect got in the way of seeing. Straddling the narrow stream, Tom kept his hands near his ankles, ready to move like greased lightning and grab a slippery specimen.

Tom searched for the dusky, the two-lined or striped salamander, and the purple salamander. The dusky had a broad yellow stripe down its back and liked the stream edges, spongy moist banks, and wet leaves.

The purple salamander, or "northern spring," didn't appear to match its name. As an adult its back was light yellowish brown tinged with a reddish or light salmon color. It had a rare orange form too. The hope of seeing a

Salamanders live in small pools along the rocky stream bed

rare one added to the zest of the search. Tom looked for this salamander in the really cold, faster-running water.

As the two intruders moved upstream, Tom's hand zipped out and caught a purple salamander. Its intestine showed through its skin. Even this one was not common. It was a lucky find and Tom was pleased. He hoped to do a metabolic study. There was not a lot of information available about these creatures. There were not good life histories because the salamanders were so hard to find. Tom partially filled a plastic bag with stream water and slipped in the salamander.

A cobbler's apron tied around Tom's waist held all his equipment and the bagged salamander. The apron freed both his hands. And two hands were needed for this job. Tom was a contortionist. Bent in half, with his head almost to his toes and his eyes at stream level, he operated both his hands at the same time, turning rocks. He had developed his skill with lots of practice and some falls. Hurt knees and sprained ankles when a foot slipped on a rock seemed to be hazards of the profession.

Pat's back tired from bending over for so long a time. She moved like an ape, hands in front of her feet as she turned stones up the stream bed. More than one salamander slipped through her fingers. As she tried to catch a red-backed, her fingers caught between two rocks—another hazard.

The red-backed had two black stripes on either side of the broad red band down the middle of its back. The escaped red-backed was a terrestrial, or land, form, but remained where it was damp and where more prey lived. There were about twenty thousand red-backed in the study area. These salamanders were not to be confused with the bigger reddish newt in Mirror Lake.

Experience gave Tom his knack. Picking up small stones, he turned them over out of the way of larger stones. Finding pools under the turned stones, his hand gently felt the sand beneath. Edging the pool, he caught a larval form along with a handful of sand. Making a loose fist to entrap the salamander and wash the sand away, Tom showed Pat a salamander losing its gills.

Marked and unmarked larval young were discovered in the center pools. The adults were nearer the shallower edge of the pools, because their skin was used for breathing air.

In this narrow stream there was less chance for adults. The day before, Tom had worked the stream from the base to the top and caught 105 adults.

Under a rock in the stream twenty eggs rested across the neck of a female with her head under the water. A slime that might be an antibiotic seemed to keep down disease for a week or more after hatching. In other observations Tom found the two-lined salamander clutch size to be thirty-two to thirty-three eggs, higher than previously reported. The nests were in riffle areas or at the stream edge in quiet waters.

As the two stream striders rested to straighten their backs and catch their breath, Tom pointed out a crane-fly larva with a number of extensions on its breathing tubes called spiracles. This crane fly might become part of some salamander's meal, joining snails, mites, worms, and other detritus eaters. Invertebrates rich in calcium, like the snails and mites, may be necessary parts of a salamander's diet. A higher concentration of calcium was found in the salamanders than in most of the invertebrates on which they fed. The salamanders appeared to concentrate calcium.

Tom pointed out the larval form of a caddis fly on the underside of a rock. It had made a protective case from straw, sand grains, and wood. Moving around the stream, it ate dead leaves. This detritivore, or detritus eater, might be another snack for a salamander larva.

Tom told Pat that up to half the salamanders might be killed by freezing. Others were eaten. After two years as a larval form in the water, a salamander might reach the average age of five. If it was lucky, it might become an oldster of ten years.

As they started salamandering again, Pat was quick and caught a dusky close to three inches long—75mm. by Tom's measure. Tom aged salamanders by their size and testis development.

Following Tom was like going through a fun house. Logs, debris, and large boulders in the stream had to be climbed, skirted, or squeezed under and through. Once such an obstacle held a downy surprise—one very upset adult junco chirped angrily at Tom and Pat. Looking closely at the tangle of roots that dangled from the uprooted tree, they spotted the cause for the alarm. Four soft balls of gray fluff with four sets of black, staring eyes and four yellow-striped mouths. Tick, tick, tick! Mother junco scolded! The two intruders withdrew.

Focusing her eyes on something other than the stream, Pat looked around. A little white oxalis blossom with pink lines drawn on delicate white petals brightened the bank. An American toad, *Bufo americanus,* croaked at them. A wasp nest on the stem of a downed beech spelled danger. A deerfly with its red nose and black spots on translucent wings bit the herpetologists with as much vigor as it bit the ornithologists. A crane fly, the caddis flies, some swarming black flies, and several house flies buzzed busily around, while a water strider walked on top of the water.

By noon they had caught 36 salamanders. Six were already marked. The ratio of marked to captured would give Tom a decimal percentage (p) to use along with the number of salamanders he had originally marked (M) to plug into the Peterson or Lincoln Index to give him the number (N) for the population of the pool he had sampled: $N = \frac{M}{p}$. This mark and recapture technique was used by many of the researchers discovering the animal populations for the community they studied.

Turning stones ended as the stream trickled out to nothing at its source. Tom had captured, marked, and put the salamanders back into the stream. Another day some of the ones he had marked this day would be recaptured along with more unmarked individuals.

Specimens he wished to examine more closely or to test stayed moist in their plastic bags partially filled with stream water.

Hiking back to the car, Tom explained that the strip-cut next to the woods that shaded the salamander stream was designed to favor yellow birch regrowth. Prize birch needed shade to regenerate and win the competition with other invading species such as the sun lovers, beech and maple. Between the strip-cuts, double widths of forest were left for shade—80-foot cut strip, 160-foot forest strip, and so on. In a few years they could tell whether the pattern did produce the birch they wanted.

Back at the farmhouse lab, Tom injected a 10 percent formalin solution into the salamander bodies with syringe and needle. After several days he rinsed them and put them in 70 percent ethyl alcohol in gallon-size glass jars.

By the end of his summers of work Tom's data told him some new facts about salamander roles in the forest ecosystem. His doctoral dissertation reported his findings.

The terrestrial red-backed *(P. cinereus)* made up 93 percent of the salamander biomass. *P. cinereus* numbered about 2,600 per hectare. The other 7 percent of the salamanders stayed near streams. Since salamanders stayed around one area, a restricted home range, they were not important as transporters of nutrients into or out of the ecosystem.

Tom thought the salamander's biggest job, or primary role, was moving nutrients within the ecosystem itself, or "intrasystem cycling." Salamanders appeared to regulate the invertebrate populations in the ground litter. The detritivores were the salamander's prey. These were the invertebrate creatures that broke down the litter into smaller and smaller pieces.

Being the top predator in the detritivore food web, the salamanders helped keep alive many different kinds of smaller prey. This diversity led to a more complete breakdown of the litter. Tom reasoned that any increase in the breakdown of the litter made more of the nutrients in the nutrient pool available to the growing plants. This chain—litter, detritivore breaking down litter, more nutrients available to plants—could have some regulating effect on the workings of the ecosystem.

Salamanders were not very important to the energy flow in the ecosystem. They used only .02 to .03 percent of the total energy or calories produced by the green plants.

Of each 8 kilocalories of energy that flowed through the salamander populations, 5 made new salamander tissue and 3 were lost from the ecosystem as respiration.

Tom compared his salamander energy flow to what the bird and mammal investigators had discovered. Salamanders used only 20 percent as much energy as the amount that flowed through bird populations. Birds do not make much flesh with their energy—they use their energy for heat and movements like flight. Salamanders make efficient use of their food. Sixty percent of their ingested energy goes into new tissue.

Salamanders also use less energy for the amount of flesh produced than mammals do. Since birds and mammals are warm-blooded and must maintain body temperatures, they are less efficient in their use of energy. Tom reasoned that the salamanders would be a better source of energy for their predators and offer more protein than birds and mammals.

The Hubbard Brook salamanders were one of the prime food sources of the garter snake, *Thamnophis s. sirtalis.* They were also a small part of the diet of shrews and ground-foraging birds like the thrushes.

Except maybe, for sodium and calcium, salamanders were not "sinks" in the intra-ecosystem nutrient cycles. Salamanders did not horde or build up and keep in their bodies any particular chemicals.

The salamanders appeared to have a stable population. Their biomass was twice the biomass of birds during the bird's peak breeding season and about equal to small mammals.

Tom examined the stomachs of some of his salamanders and identified twenty-nine different kinds of prey. He identified the insects and other detritivores himself.

To be an ecologist, Tom had to be a jack-of-all-trades. He had to be able to learn to do new things.

12

SUPERSPY: THE MAMMALOGIST

"I had it all," Gary was quick to admit. "Gray flannel suit, tie, neat handkerchief in the pocket."

Why did Gary give up his well-paid job in aerospace? Why did he exchange his fancy clothes, house, furniture, and parties for the barely-make-ends-meet salary of a graduate assistant?

Gary was not among those students nominated as the "person most likely to succeed" in high school. According to him he would have been voted "most unlikely to succeed." He was advised to avoid college. But Gary liked a challenge. His attitudes changed. He completed college and won a job that amazed his former classmates.

But this was not the ending point for Gary. Inside all day in a physiology lab or behind a typewriter writing up his research, he remembered the science field methods course he had taken from Dick. Gary had taken it just for fun, not as part of his program of work. But it had been the course he had most enjoyed in college. Gradually he realized he liked working in the outdoors.

Gary's bubbly enthusiasm, eagerness, drive, and energetic ability to play or work equally hard were now channeled toward a new goal—outdoor research and a doctoral degree.

So he moved his family to Dartmouth in Hanover, New Hampshire, and began five years of preparation to be either a college professor who did field research or a year-round researcher.

Once his goals were set, work became his play. The hairy and furry warm-blooded mammals didn't have a chance to keep their activities and whereabouts a secret any longer. Gary, the supersleuth, was on the scene to spy on them.

Like most self-confident, eager-beaver graduate students, Gary's first research goals were too large. He had to limit his study. Instead of getting quantitative data on most of the mammals, Gary was guided to select a few.

First, he sampled the area to see what was present. From thirty or forty acres, he chose fourteen acres for removal grids and trapping. From his findings, he decided to study the northern jumping mouse, the deer mouse, and the Boreal red-backed vole.

He wanted to learn the number of each species in the ecosystem. And he wanted to learn what part of the standing crop of nutrients in the forest rested in these three species. He worked out annual energy budgets for each species. He wanted to know how much energy flowed through the mouse populations. He also hoped to learn whether their seed-eating habits affected the trees.

Dr. Likens' lab chemists analyzed Gary's mammal specimens for the same elements as the other organisms and water samples from the forest: N, Ca, P, K, Na, Mg, Fe, Zn, Mn, and Cu. Lead, copper, and cadmium, heavy elements, were added to Gary's analysis list. These elements might concentrate in small mammals.

He listed other mammals as he accidentally discovered them. In this way a species list grew.

To make his census he set out live traps on a grid with one hundred stations twenty-five meters apart. He marked the animals in a variety of patterns to identify captured individuals and to be able to recognize them when they were recaptured.

To check the accuracy of his live-trap census, Gary planned to snap-trap and compare the numbers.

With either trapping method, weather was a dictator. Rain told Gary to hurry out to his live traps. He freed trapped animals so they wouldn't suffer from exposure. He released the traps so no animal would get caught. Rain tripped snap traps. Trapped raindrops did not add up to representative sampling.

Gary used a Sherman collapsible live trap which was made from shiny sheet aluminum. It was 2½ x 3 x 8½ inches large. He set the door open and baited the back room. A mouse running in stepped on the treadle and the door snapped closed. To retrieve the animal Gary opened the other end of the trap.

At his grid stations traps were set for three rainless nights. The mice were caught and marked. Other trespassers were released and described in

Gary's journal. The next eight to twelve days the traps weren't set. Then for three more days the traps were set. The cycle was repeated several more times.

A museum special spring trap snapped out an area. It looked like a large version of a house mousetrap. The larger size saved skulls from being crushed. The museum special took larger mice too. Any properly prepared mammal specimen must be accompanied by a cleaned skull for proper species identification.

Gary prebaited for three days without setting the traps. Then he baited and set the traps for five days. The number of individuals trapped went down each night. When the individuals trapped reached a low point, he knew most of the area was trapped out. Then he knew approximately the number present. At the end of the live-trap censusing, Gary snap-trapped the two and a half acres in the middle of the live-trap census area. Then he compared results, checking his live-trap numbers with his snap-trap numbers.

Getting a mammal count was a tough job. Numbers changed a lot from place to place, hour to hour, and season to season. Since very different sets of numbers came from the same plot, many numbers were needed before a real idea of a population's parameters—the most and least number of mice that might be present—could be obtained. Few samples would give the wrong idea. So a lot of trapping was necessary in one place.

Gary found the population estimate from the recapture technique very close to his snap-trap removal numbers. His censusing data were, then, fairly close to the actual number of mice in the forest.

Even though he was getting the numbers he needed, Gary was puzzled by the distribution of the small mammals. In one habitat that looked the same as the others, he found mammals in some parts, but not in others. The mice were not evenly distributed. Gary did not know why. That might be a puzzle for another researcher to work out someday.

Some of the live-trapped mammals went to the Dartmouth lab where the amount of oxygen they used was measured. The oxygen consumption showed their metabolism rate, or how much energy the animal used just to stay alive, at different temperatures.

Gary multiplied his total number of animals by the average energy used by the individuals. This told him the minimum amount of energy used by his mouse populations.

On a dining table in the farmhouse, Gary opened his tackle box of skinning equipment. Mammals were preserved in the same way as birds—skinned and stuffed.

Gary experimented to perfect his skin study technique. Scissor tips cut through the lower abdomen and up the chest to open a pocket of skin and fur. Thumbs and fingers gently pulled the pelt away from the body sack tissue that held all the inner organs. Gary turned the mouse's coat inside out as it slipped away from the body. Snips around the ankles, eyes, ears, nose, and mouth allowed the skin coat to slide off the mouse. While the fur coat was turned inside out, Gary rubbed it in a mixture of borax and arsenic (cornmeal can also be used) to absorb body moisture. Around a loop of heavy wire, Gary wound cotton batting and pressed it into a shape that matched the removed body. Wires were pushed inside each foot, making it straight for drying. Gary became adept with a needle and thread. He neatly sewed together the chest opening. He pushed, pressed, squeezed. Soon a study skin was ready for a museum tray.

Behind the mounted animals displayed in a public museum are the museum's working collection of study skins. Museum trays are stacked and pulled out like drawers. A series of the same species is grouped together so variations can be compared. Many colleges have their own collections of study skins. Gary could take his skins to a museum for comparison. Maybe he had an unusual species for the area. His study skin could be compared to an identified specimen and become proof of a capture.

Museums trade specimens. Each wants as complete a series of each animal as possible. To help keep the specimens from being destroyed by insects and other vermin, paradichlorobenzene is placed in the trays. The skins are protected in the same way that moth crystals protect your woolen clothing.

Like all the other researchers, Gary kept a journal of daily field happenings and discoveries. He flipped the pages of his notebook and spotted chipmunk, deer, bear, weasels, fisher, fox (red male plus blond female and two kits), and 1 male porcupine—road kill. The date, time, location, weather and other special environmental conditions were next to each entry. Many of the notations brought to mind experiences that made good stories and would not be quickly forgotten.

Busily engrossed in his trapline, Gary once baited the trigger of a trap with a peanut butter and oats mixture. Gently he placed the trap among the leaves on the ground. He was too busy keeping his finger from being snapped to be aware of anything around him. Besides, it was cloudy and very dark. A misty cloud closed in, putting him in a fog. Startled by a limb breaking near him, he looked up. He was dead center in the path of a nearsighted bear! The bear lumbered down the hill straight toward Gary. Gary waved his arms, yelled and shouted, trying to scare him off. But the bear kept coming straight on course. With the bear's momentum, he might not have been able to veer off even if Gary had scared him. Anyway, Gary didn't pose much of a threat. At the last moment he jumped to avoid a head-to-chest collision and landed sitting in a stream. Unaware, the bear lumbered down the hillside at the same brash pace. A short ten feet had separated them.

One rainy night while Gary and Tom rooted in the salamander transect plots, an unknown assailant landed, thump, on Tom's chest and held on tightly. Light from his flashlight flickered in all directions through the forest trees as Tom tried to pull off his unseen assailant. Trying to get rid of his attacker, he ran through the forest. Gary ran after Tom, finally spotting the assailant with his flashlight. A flying squirrel had landed square on Tom's chest. It must have been a shock for the squirrel too. How many trees could have run away with it in the past? Once in the spotlight, the squirrel sailed off and Tom's heartbeat returned slowly to normal.

Gary and Dot checked his live-trap line one morning. Gary took two tiny, long-snouted mouselike miniatures out of his trap. The shrews had black, soft velvet fur. Their fur had no nap. It lay down flat against their bodies either way Dot smoothed it. Napless animals like the mole and shrew can run into a hole and back out without having their fur stand up and block their exit. They are two-way animals in a hole. Their fur helps them escape their predators.

Shrews move quickly. Their small bodies lose heat rapidly. They use lots of calories and have to eat constantly to stay alive. Gary released them to continue their busy search for insects. They hadn't known Gary was trapping only mice.

Gary had just finished his shrew notes when he heard a death-defying scream. Dot was in trouble! Running to the next trap, he found her irrationally yelling, "Help, help!" Gary thought she'd gone "over the brink." He had never seen anyone so close to hysteria.

"Get'm out, get'm out!" she yelled. "He's clinging, here." Dot pointed to the crotch of her trousers. "Help me. He'll bite!"

Gary's hand beat the empty air, helplessly. "Take'm off, take'm off," he yelled.

The conflict between immediately helping his screaming friend and flashing mental images of jeanless Dot caused him to freeze. How would he explain the scene to a professor walking through the forest? Clawing the air, all he could say was, "Get'm off, get'm off!"

The mouse itself solved the problem by running down Dot's other pant leg and disappearing into the forest.

Back at the farmhouse, Dot was quiet and a bit pale. She wondered how she would have explained it all to a doctor if she had needed a tetanus shot.

Gary's notes did not tell a lot of things he remembered.

Gary could not limit himself to small mammals. On his back watching a bird one morning, he fell asleep. When he awoke, there was a neatly coiled garter snake under his head acting as his pillow!

Another day he walked into a wasp nest chest-high on a beech tree. With one wasp sting on his arm, he ran down the slope. His wicker basket pack pounded against his back. He hoped the nest hadn't fallen into the basket with the wasps readying themselves for the "big sting" when he stopped running. Gasping for breath, Gary dropped his pack, relieved to find no wasp nest.

Never to be forgotten was the eerie quiet and pitch black before a rainstorm. The lightning crackled and changed the forest to daylight for an instant, then back to a black, lightless box. Not a mouse, not a leaf stirred. Not an animal breathed or a frass fell. This strange total quiet Gary held deep in his memory.

Snow brought a clean unclutteredness to the forest and new experiences to Gary, who kept up with mammal happenings in winter as well as summer.

Snowshoes and cross-country skis took Gary wherever he wanted to go. Sometimes he went too rapidly! Once he came to an icy trough. He slid up one side, then down and up the other, out of control. Straddling the trough, he flew down the icy slide. Trying to keep his balance, he skied on his head. Finally he collapsed in a heap. Fortunately no bones were broken. The field life of a mammalogist does not always slide smoothly.

Missing the winter show were the jumping mice and chipmunks, comfortably hibernating under the snow.

Snap traps bit Gary more than once under an early snowfall or late spring surprise snowstorm. He would grapple for the trap under the snow and, zing, a finger was trapped.

Gary tried to help the mice by giving them nest boxes ten feet off the ground. When the snow fell, he checked the boxes. But no mice, only spiders. Foiled again!

Mice, foxes, and snowshoe rabbits left neat footprints on the snow. Gary entertained himself in the winter solitude by reading the stories of recent events printed on the cold white page. Fox tracks that led from a partly eaten muskrat told him the familiar predatory-prey story.

Gary, like the other graduate students, eventually counted enough animals. He was able to work out the population, the nutrient content, the biomass expressed as kilograms per hectare, and the energy consumption expressed as calories per hectare for each species he studied.

He compared his results with the ornithology and herpetology figures. He found that mammals have more biomass than birds in this forest ecosystem. But they have less than salamanders. The mammals used more energy than salamanders, but less than birds.

Gary found that the small mammals he studied were good prey, or energy source, for other organisms higher up on the food chain in the Hubbard Brook ecosystem.

The small mammal seed-eating habits did not affect the major tree species. The forest invertebrates were not affected by small mammal predation either.

Gary has reached another goal. His doctorate behind him, he seeks new goals and adventures. He will make things happen wherever he is. And the most unusual, unpredictable happenings will make new stories germinate and grow.

13

THE BIG PICTURE

More and more puzzle pieces fell into place by the end of each summer's fieldwork. A picture formed that showed the control forest close to a steady state. The forest had only slow gains of energy and biomass. The forest bank account was still increasing biomass the way your dollars left in the bank gather interest. The dead components of the forest were broken down and released to the soil at about the same rate that plants made new biomass. Nutrients cycled at the same rate that decomposing biomass gave chemical building blocks back to the soil. New rock released about the same amount of chemicals to the soil as forest streams carried out of the ecosystem. As the endless chain of nutrients revolved, dust and rain added significant amounts of new materials to this ecosystem.

A low amount of materials ran out of the ecosystem in the streams compared to runoff in other forests. But enough organic matter escaped to aid aquatic food webs that formed downstream in the black shadows of trees and bushes.

So the control forest held its own and slowly grew more biomass. More nitrogen was found to enter than to leave this undisturbed drainage basin.

On the other hand, the experimental clear-cut community, sprayed to prevent trees and shrubs from growing, was not holding its own. The researchers learned that cutting increased the removal of nitrogen. Over five times as much nitrate was found in the experimental clear-cut streams as had been in the same streams before cutting. With the loss of living root systems to anchor the soil and with the pull of gravity, some soil crept down the slopes. Soil and nutrients were lost in solution as rain and stream waters flowed down the hillsides. There was much more nutrient loss after clear-cutting. The energy-holding organic matter and the nutrient chemical account went down. One experimental area had been cut and sprayed to prevent regrowth immediately, while the other had been cut and allowed to regrow naturally. Though the control forest gained nitrogen, both experimental cut areas lost nitrogen from their ecosystems.

Perhaps the nitrogen-fixing microbes were more active and fixed more nitrogen in a cut-over area. Or, root exudates from living plants might have controlled the number of bacteria or the amount of nitrogen the microbes fixed in the soil. Maybe the plants in the control forest consumed more and held more nitrogen than in a cut-over area. Some, part, or all of these ideas might be true—maybe none. Why were the cut-over areas losing more nitrogen by way of the streams? More data and information was needed. Results often raised new problems to be solved.

In experimental areas where the natural regrowth had not been delayed after a clear-cut, there was an increase in the biomass when the second succession of plants grew. The bank account got big deposits of "the green." Nutrients and energy increased at a rapid rate. Here the ecosystem was in an unstable, rapidly increasing state.

The clear-cut was the "real" experiment, but descriptive base lines had to be discovered before the changes made by cutting showed up. You couldn't know how much more or less it rained at your house this year than last by making only this year's measurements. You have to know last year's rainfall measurement too. That measurement would be your base line for comparing this year's measurement.

By each summer's end the investigators had made more base-line measurements. They had got numbers that could be put into formulas and translated into computer language. They had changed their species counting numbers into biomass, energy, and nutrient measurements. Now such items as amphibians, mammals, birds, and plants—unlike things—could be compared.

Suppose you and a friend wanted to know who had the most groceries. How would you compare? You might change the groceries into dollars and compare their cost. Or if you wanted to compare the quantity, you could change unlike things like apples, milk, and cereal into pounds and ounces. Or each of you might burn your groceries and measure the heat in calories. Then you could see who had had the most potential energy in his shopping bag. Changing unlike things into a common measurement is what many of the researchers did.

The scientists figured out the weight, or biomass, in grams per hectare of the organisms they studied. They figured out the number of calories in each organism's biomass and the number of calories used by the organism

Clear-cut strip with trees left to shade stream

to live. Then they compared their unlike organisms in grams per hectare and calories per square meter.

Birds had less biomass than salamanders or mammals in the forest. But more energy, measured as calories, passed through the bird community. The birders had measured the amount of energy the birds used by measuring their respiration in the laboratory and their activity in the forest. Birds burned a lot of calories to live.

The researchers had a lot of information. They figured out the amount of energy that flowed through certain individual populations of plants and animals. They measured much of the potential energy tied up as biomass in the ecosystem. They measured the new nutrients that entered the ecosystem with the rainfall or that were released from the existing rocks.

Many of the steps in the nutrient cycle and energy flow had numbers that showed how much of the forest's energy and nutrients were in or used by each member of the Hubbard Brook ecosystem. Scientists had studied the nutrients as they cycled from the ground into plants then into animals. Nutrients moved along food chains to dead animals and detritus that was broken down by small microscopic organisms. Nutrients finally returned to the soil to be recycled into plants, and so the endless chain went round and round.

Some of the nutrients moved out of the ecosystem by way of streams or the territorial wanderings of the animals. But nutrients and energy taken from the ecosystem by departing animals such as the birds and bats were balanced by those brought in with animals entering the ecosystem boundary. And so territorial wandering and migration losses were regained seasonally. The control forest neared a steady state.

14

DATA, DATA, DATA

From the six small watersheds came a lot of data: Water input and output was measured. Chemical input and output was figured. Particulate gains and losses were counted. Energy budgets for several organisms and the litter were charted. Temperatures of the streams, soil, and lake were recorded. Nutrients in the soil and organisms were recorded, and so on and on—data, data, data, everywhere. Where did all these numbers go?

Each researcher had his own private field notes and journals filled with data. Records of the chemical analyses that were done at the Cornell Ecology Laboratory were kept in several forms.

Field sheets of "on the spot" observations and measurements were kept in thick blue-binder notebooks, all labeled by date with black marking pen. Blue-binder notebooks filled shelf after shelf and represented about $1,200,000 in data. Eleven years of records made a lot of data!

From the information in the blue notebooks IBM punch cards were filled out for each sample analyzed. These data included such things as temperature, conductivity (electrical), as well as the chemical content of the sample and other information from the original field sheets.

Each day it rained, the new data were added and run through the computer for continuous monthly totals and average concentrations of chemicals by the month and year. Until IBM cards were used, data were recorded as raised dots on narrow white rolls of paper tape.

The IBM machine quickly sorted large batches of information when the searchers knew what information they wanted. But as handy as the IBM computer cards were for getting at specific data, they were not easy to browse through for general ideas and new questions to ask. The original field sheets continued to have a separate purpose as a source of readable information. The blue binders filled with field observations ensured future investigators data that might answer new questions as yet unasked and unimagined.

Other materials available for future projects and for checking on old project results were water samples in clear plastic bottles. Rooms with floor-to-ceiling shelves were filled with plastic bottles. Labeled with a permanent black marking pen when they were collected, the water samples were the basis for the thousands of observations recorded as data in the blue notebooks and on the IBM cards. The estimated cost of each bottle was five dollars. This cost included the labor to obtain, test, and record the data for the sample.

The bird, insect, plant, salamander, litter, water, root exudate, and other analyses all depended on special analyzing machines at the Cornell Ecology Laboratory. The Hubbard Brook project would have been almost impossible before an Australian machine, the autoanalyzer, was invented. Cornell had received the fifteenth machine in the United States. This ingenious invention made it possible for one lab technician to operate and quickly record data from water analysis for thirty-two chemicals. For eleven years weekly water samples had been analyzed without a break. In the past it would have taken a lab technician hours to do the same analyses on one bottle of water.

Another machine, the atomic absorption spectrophotometer, burned a sample. The color of the flame indicated the kind of gaseous elements present and their amounts in milligrams. Dials were read by the lab technician, who recorded the chemical contents on data sheets and then punched out the information on IBM cards.

Dependent on these machines for processing their data, the researchers were also dependent on the skill of the technicians who kept them in working order.

Throughout the history of science, new devices have allowed scientists to extend their data-gathering ability. Frequently new equipment must be tried and compared to equipment in present use.

For a while "Erni" kept Dr. Likens company in his office. Looking like any normal friendly household robot, Erni opened automatically when it rained. He was put out to pasture side by side with two other rain collectors in an enclosed experimental yard. Erni, with a chemist checking, not only measured rain, but immediately recorded the pesticides and other chemicals present in the rainwater. Will an Erni someday monitor our yards?

Hubbard Brook data also went to Yale University and into a program for a computer. By using IBM cards filled with Hubbard Brook facts, the computer predicted in picture form the appearance of the Hubbard Brook Forest in any given number of years—five, ten, one hundred, five hundred, etc. By using data such as plant species biomass as the basis for expected growth rates, the computer mimicked forest growth, showing height, mass, and density the way a television cartoon mimicks real-life events. The computer can show in picture form the growth and death of a mature Hubbard Brook Forest, given different treatments.

Another seeable product of data-gathering in the woods was stored behind metal doors at the Cornell Ecology Lab. The shelves were piled with reprints of many journal articles written about the Hubbard Brook research projects. Interested scientists wanted their own copies to learn about methods used, data obtained, or results reached in a project.

After fieldwork was finished, data gathered, and numbers recorded and translated to IBM cards, charts, and graphs, memories remained. Researcher's memories of their fieldwork were often different from their published reports. Memories stored the curious, interesting, and humorous angles of a project.

Dr. Likens and Dr. Margaret Davis' crew chuckled when they remembered how they had moved the 12½-meter lake cores. The mud cores were cut into 780–830 centimeter lengths, wrapped in plastic and foil, and placed in aluminum rain gutters for protection during their ride to Dr. Davis' freezer.

"What if a policeman stopped her on the way home?" the researchers asked jokingly. "Would he believe her story of wrapped mud? Would the police think she was a criminal trying to hide something? After all, who carries neatly wrapped mud in the trunk of his car? A likely story!"

Those same mud cores kept Dr. Davis busy for several years in her laboratory. While uncovering the history of Mirror Lake she came upon another nature mystery.

About five thousand years ago, the lake was surrounded by a spruce forest that must have been destroyed suddenly and completely. The lake showed extreme productivity during one period of its life. But after a certain date no more of the spruce pollen appeared in the mud core slices. What had happened? Fire? A heavy snowstorm? Some mysteries remained mysteries.

The insect researchers remembered their first study year, when *Heterocampa* caterpillars appeared in large enough numbers to "eat up" a forest. In many places the caterpillar seemed to be doing just that. But as predicted, *Heterocampa* numbers crashed. The forest survived, but the number of young birds that were fledged declined. Migration returns were fewer, and fewer young birds appeared in the forest when the *Heterocampa* numbers were down. There was less food for the young birds.

Observers decided that insect parasites reduced the *Heterocampa* numbers in their cyclic rise and sudden fall of population. *Heterocampa,* the bird food, controlled the number of fledglings able to survive in the forest, rather than the birds' controlling the number of *Heterocampa.* When birds ate *Heterocampa* caterpillars, it just looked as if birds were controlling this insect. A scientist can't always believe his eyes. That's why he counts and analyzes his data.

The bird people had their special memories. One year observers saw great numbers of scarlet tanagers dead on roadways. It seemed as if their whole population had suffered mass death. What caused the tragedy?

A late cold snap with a steady rain arrived with the birds migrating to the northern woods from their southerly winter feeding areas. Their strength and food reserves were all gone from their long flight. Stomach samples showed signs of starvation. Leaves and twigs were found in tanager stomachs, showing that none of their usual insect food was available. The cold killed the insects, and the tanagers, next to them in a food chain, starved.

In years to come, would tanager numbers begin to rise? Practically unseen in the forest, a few managed to survive and reproduce themselves. A few young added to the small population might make the breed visible in a number of years. Downy woodpecker, nuthatch, and chickadee numbers had been lower for several years after a late winter freezing rain. Their population had slowly increased again. Would the tanagers? The researchers watched and counted. These interrelationships and nature mysteries make the ecologists' work exciting.

The botanists had their finds too. The pin cherry, identified by white streaks on reddish bark, was a pioneer plant. As a pioneer species it prepared the way for the young plants of a climax forest that would again shade newly buried pin cherry seeds. If fire, snow, or man destroyed the forest, the pin cherry would be ready to spring up and hold the soil and help a new forest grow. These kinds of interrelationships between the community and its physical environment fascinated the ecologists.

Ecology is not something discovered and known. At Hubbard Brook new interrelationships were being discovered all the time and known interrelationships were changing too, just the way people purposefully and forcefully change their own environments.

The professors' measurements from the weather stations and rainwater analyses showed that environmental clean-up efforts must be monitored. They discovered that the results of good intentions and actions are not always as expected.

Measurements showed a decrease in soot and ash as local manufacturers and homes changed from coal to cleaner natural gas fuel. There was 70 percent less sulfur in the rainwater than before 1950. Pollution controls appeared to be working.

When coal was used, sulfur fell to the ground near its burning site as neutral salts. Now pollution control devices, like screens, trap particles, many of which are alkaline. New taller smokestacks send sulfur dioxide gas into the air much higher up than coal burner stacks. Sulfur dioxide may spread farther out over a bigger area. Researchers have suggested that without the alkaline particles in the air to neutralize the acids, the sulfur changes into an acid and stays acid. This may account for the gradual increase in the amount of acid rain that has fallen on the Hubbard Brook Forest over the last twenty years in spite of the soot control devices. The next step will be to control sulfur oxides.

Rain and snow have a neutral acid value. Northeast rains measured had more acid than other places. Some storms measured as acid as the vinegar you buy in the grocery store. Acid rain leaches nutrients from the plants and perhaps the soil. Acid rains and snows may have held back forest growth in the last twenty years.

Too much acidity kills fish, wears away public buildings and statues. Wheelbarrows and tools left out in acid rains wear away more quickly. Acid rain costs us all in many ways.

The pine trees in some spots of the San Gabriel Mountains in southern California were dying. Could it have been the warm, heated air rising from the sulfur-dioxide-filled valley below? Suppose you breathed this kind of air every day—what might happen to your lungs? The researchers at Hubbard Brook may help ring warning bells that will help us change our ways and save ourselves along with our environment.

For the basic scientist, a study doesn't have to have an immediate practical use. Learning more about what and how things happen in the world is reason enough. But as a spin-off, ecologists studying food chains have learned how the poisons used on farms and lawns made their way into water systems, entered the nutrient system of the tiny phytoplankton, were eaten by the zooplankton and continued to concentrate up the food chain, finally killing fish and birds. There may be only a little poison in each microscopic animal in the lake, but if one fish eats many such animals, that one fish is going to contain a lot more poison than the smaller animal. In this way poison builds up or concentrates at each higher level in the food chain. Fish are killed. Birds that feed on fish get more poison in their bodies. The poison upsets their ability to make eggshells. Their soft eggshells don't protect the new bird. No birds like peregrine falcons or bald eagles hatch from soft-shelled eggs. When the food chains of all the peregrines or bald eagles contain enough poison, no egg may hatch. At that moment a species will become extinct, and "extinct is forever."

What happens in the human body that eats fish and other animals containing concentrated poisons? Scientists are continuing to try to find answers to that question. We ourselves are guinea pigs.

Just by existing, the animals in the world play a role in the community of the ecosystems where they live. Man may not always understand the role of each animal until it is gone. And although other animal species as well as humans should not have to prove their right to continue life in our ecosystem, the earth, they do have a purpose to human welfare. If the earth is healthy enough to sustain a variety of plants and animals, it will be a healthy enough environment to sustain human life too. If the environment cannot sustain varied animal life, the human race may find itself an endangered species. Variety in the organism world is necessary for the continuance of life.

Feeding the multitudes may someday be considered another problem for the ecologists to solve. There are many systems at work to get food to hungry people.

Land recently taken out of America's land bank became rich with nutrients as it lay resting for years. It is fertile land, ready to grow good crops.

After several seasons of crops, fertilizers will be needed to put back into the soil the chemicals taken by the plants. Then food prices may go up, because we are running out of inexpensive fertilizers. It takes oil to ship raw fertilizer-making materials to places like Florida, where ten percent of the state's electrical energy is now used to change raw material—much of it also petroleum—into the farmer's needed fertilizers.

After food is grown it must be transported to where it is needed. More fuel and energy are used to transport the food. Fuel is limited and expensive. Some people will not have food because it cannot be transported to them.

With the computer, more data, and continuing study, the ecologist may be able to prescribe, like the medical doctor who is consulted by a sick patient. He may diagnose the carrying capacity of the earth and suggest reasonable distributions of populations near food sources. He may indicate lands best suited to crops so that good land will not become cemented roadways or covered with houses. He might suggest locations for homes that would be less likely to stand in the way of expected natural disasters like floods and mud slides.

But in all cases, like the physician, the ecologist will be a consultant. Governments and individuals will have to decide whether or not to follow the ecology doctor's advice, fill his prescriptions, and take the necessary medicine.

The ecologist cannot and will not make our value judgments for us. Each of us, as individuals and parts of groups, must make our own decisions and vote accordingly. The ecologists can only tell us what exists and what might happen when we decide to act in certain ways. Societies will make the value judgments—the scientist will only provide information to help us make our choices.

15

ENDINGS AND BEGINNINGS

As projects at Hubbard Brook were completed, more written reports lined college library shelves. Newly turned out researchers left the Brook. Some members of the team began a lifetime of research. Others became science teachers and researchers at universities, small colleges, and high schools.

Several Hubbard Brook "alumni" began newly created jobs in the outdoors as field researchers for private firms and Government agencies. A few students had the opportunity to become ecology synthesizers, writing ecological reports for the new and old organizations required to make impact statements to the Government. The "synthesizer" takes all the field research data and brings the information together in a meaningful way. Synthesizers analyze the facts and write reports that offer recommendations for future actions. Synthesizers appeared to be in demand.

Many qualified researchers do not care to be inside behind a desk all day writing impact statements. Some ecologists avoid these jobs because they feel pressure might be put on them to hurry a report to meet deadlines. They do not want to be put in a position where they might be asked to use data to support private business need or agency prejudice. The ecologists want to be free to make as accurate ecological observations and judgments as they can. A person in conflict with his ethics or principles would be an unhappy person and a discontented employee.

Business, government, and individuals may have to put first what is best, in the long run, for everyone. Science, with its data-gathering and analysis systems, is simple compared to the difficulties in changing the habits, lifestyles, values, goals, customs, ethics, and laws of people. It is easier to discover a floodplain than to get people to move from an area that is repeatedly flooded.

New steps in communication made it possible for the originators of the Hubbard Brook project to piece together a unified picture. Weekly telephone calls between Dr. Borman and Dr. Likens kept each informed of new projects under their direction and the happenings and findings of research that was under way. Each new project idea was discussed and worked out with one of the three men who had started the ecosystem research. A meeting each spring of all the people working on projects in the Brook allowed them to become acquainted with each other's objectives and methods. During the year meetings were held. Progress reports were given. As papers were written, copies were sent to each scientist working on the project. Each had a chance to make his comments.

The Hubbard Brook project resulted in a better understanding of an ecosystem. It developed a procedure for including individual projects as part of one whole study. Students and established researchers, given freedom to follow their own interests and choose their own projects, worked diligently and with dedication. Many workers were able to contribute to the accumulation of project data. Hubbard Brook successfully broke ground in cooperative ecosystem study, using nutrient cycling and energy flow research to link together the many sections of the chain of nature.

As an ecological research station, Hubbard Brook became an early model for other research areas in the U.S. and other countries. The station received many visitors interested in getting ideas for running their own ecological projects. A much larger grassland project in the Western United States was patterned after Hubbard Brook in some ways.

If enough is learned about many different habitats and the functioning of their ecosystems, scientists may be able to predict what is happening to the whole earth ecosystem. They may be able to predict what can happen according to the different treatments man might give his world.

Governments may ask for the ecologist's help in managing wisely earth's resources to best ensure a healthy, adequately fed and housed population.

Another result of the Hubbard Brook study was more questions.

After departing researchers had fitted their pieces of the Hubbard Brook puzzle into place, new puzzle players took their places. New initials appeared in the freezer and refrigerator and on the numerous boxes crowding the kitchen. New faces appeared around the dinner table, the research tables, and in the laboratories and woods. A new "Bob" took over Dave G.'s pit, the dungeon in the basement.

New steps to solve new mysteries began each summer. Three researchers used scuba equipment to search the bottom of Mirror Lake for carnivorous plants—macrophytes. Patiently Bob cleaned the green plants, placed them in aluminum foil, numbered them with a black marker and placed the twenty species he had found in the freezer. What kept them from filling the lake? Would he find their limiting factor?

How much carbon dioxide exchange occurred between the lake and the air? Bruce and his silver-painted floating dome hoped to find out.

Did wax paper and shoe boxes help Sally collect bird stomach samples after encouraging the bird to throw up?

How many species of mayflies did Sandy discover?

Did Jo Ann find the piece of the puzzle that showed why more nitrogen was lost from the clear-cut areas? Did her procedure using a hypodermic needle to inject gases and take gases from rubber-stoppered baby-food jars help her discover the nitrogen fixation rate by free living algae and bacteria? Did it help measure the rate of nitrogen fixation in the soil of a watershed?

Would the stacks of petri dishes with colorful fungi and the floating automatic water samplers help Marilyn total the respiration of everything in the lake?

Did Judy work out the phosphorus budget for her stream? How much phosphorus went in and how much came out of the watershed she studied?

Time as well as measuring, recording, and analyzing data might give them their answers.

Bruce and silver-colored dome

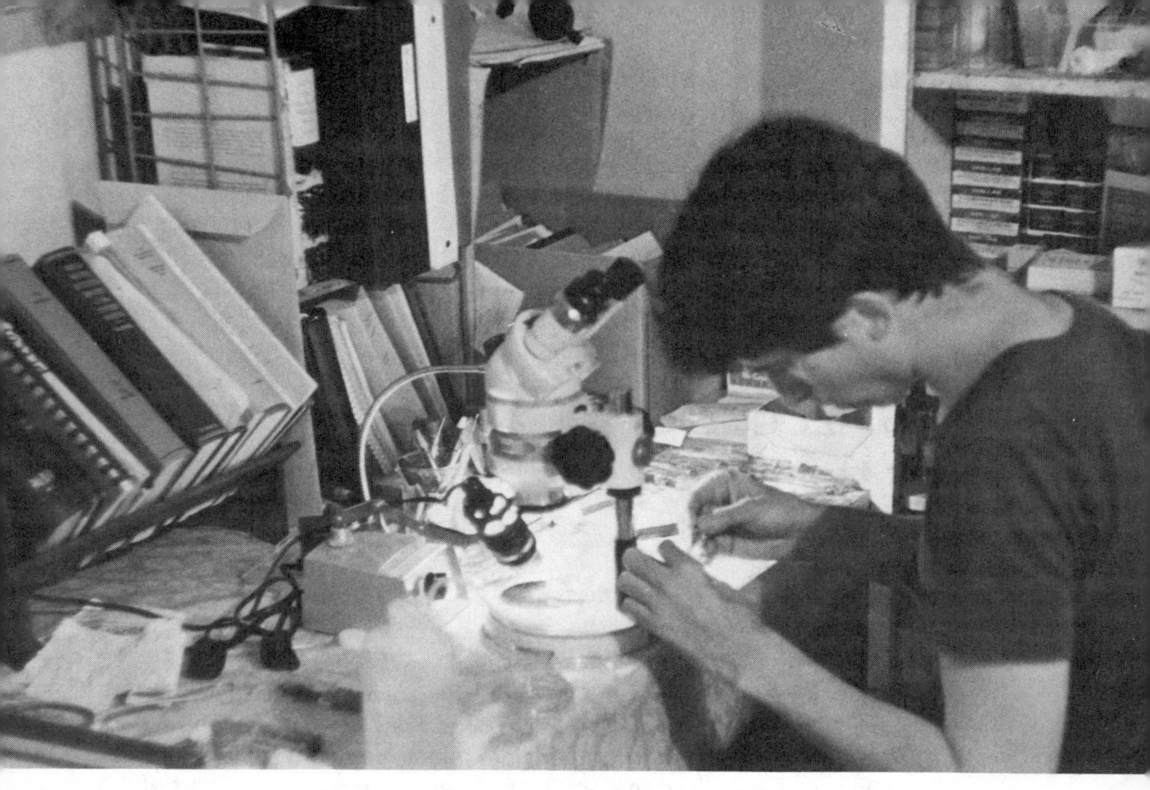

Sandy, entomology student, studies mayflies under dissecting binocular microscope

Marilyn holds apparatus for suspending dark and clear bottles in lake

16

THE ECOLOGIST AS A SCIENTIST

To find out about an environment ecologists solve their problems like all scientists. They get an idea and guess, or hypothesize, what might be true. Gary could have guessed that a certain number of mice were in the forest. He might have supposed that small mammals were not a large part of the forest biomass.

Like any scientist, the ecologist must invent ways to gather data—facts, information—that might support or refute the original hypothesis. Gary trapped the mice to count them. He had to trap them in ways that gave unbiased numbers to put into his formulas. And he had to check his data for reliability. Gary snap-trapped to check his live-trap numbers.

Scientists analyze their data and figure out what the numbers mean. Gary counted mice. Perhaps there were more than he had guessed. But he discovered that his small mammals still made only a small part of the total forest biomass. After analyzing his data, he revised his hypothesis—changed his thinking—to fit what he discovered. By comparing data he generalized that mice add more biomass to an ecosystem than birds, but less than salamanders.

Scientific experiments and descriptive science may follow this general approach to a problem. But the steps do not always follow each other in the same sequence. One step may even be left out or skipped over to get to a general conclusion. A recipe may guide a cook who substitutes and adds ingredients in a different order. But if the cook is creative, the resulting dish is tasty. The scientist's dish is new information about the world in which we live (basic science) or new knowledge about how to use the elements of our world (applied science).

Serendipity means a gift for making accidental, fortunate discoveries. A scientist may be looking for one thing and discover something else that he was not looking for at all. Serendipity plays a big role in scientific progress and has helped add many new pieces of information to ecosystem puzzles.

Another concern of all scientists is scientific ethics. A scientist must be accurate and honest as far as possible in his report of methods, measurements, and results. He cannot cheat by doctoring up measurements to turn out the way he would like them to be. Other scientists must be able to respect and depend upon a person's work or they can't use it. If a scientist is shown to be intentionally dishonest in his reporting in one instance, all the rest of his work may be suspected and unusable. All the work would have to be done over by someone with a good reputation.

What makes a person become an ecologist rather than another kind of scientist?

An ecologist is usually another kind of scientist first. He has a specialty, a deep knowledge of one scientific area. To this specialty he adds a general knowledge of all parts of the environment and the interrelationships between the parts. And so the forester, limnologist, botanist, zoologist, herpetologist, and ornithologist each becomes a scientific generalist, an ecologist.

Along with every new science comes a new vocabulary. Words convey ideas or concepts about things. If there are new ideas and new ways of seeing an old world, new words are needed to describe the new ideas. So ecologists have their own vocabulary. Some of the words may fool you. They can be common words used every day. But the ecologists have given them new meanings. A community can mean the town where you live. It can also mean all the plants and animals living in a common environment. To you a pioneer may mean a family in a covered wagon. To an ecologist it may mean an invading species—the first tree growing in a grassy meadow. The glossary at the end of this book will help you learn new meanings for old words and new ecological words too.

You and a mammalogist may know a lot about a cat and a mouse. But an ecologist may think of a cat as a predator and the mouse as prey when they are found in the same environment. Ecologists are quick to think of the relationships that exist between two or more things in an environment.

A botanist may see a pine forest. The ecologist sees a climax forest where the young trees are the same species as mature trees. He sees dead trees decaying and materials being returned to the forest system for recycling.

A geologist may see granite rock exposed by a road cut. An ecologist will see that the primary invaders of lichen and mosses attached to the granite are beginning the process of soil formation.

A vacationer will see morning sun on a green mountainside. The ecologist will see a southern exposure with drier and warmer growing conditions than a nearby northern exposure. He knows which plants can grow on the southern slope, and the plants tell him which animals may be found living in the community.

Once you put on ecologist's glasses, you do not see the world the same way any more. Your vision is clearer and wider. You see much more of the world than you did before using special glasses.

Natural history—the study of the life cycles of individual organisms and their behavior—was a stepping-stone to the science of ecology. Ecology has been referred to as "quantified natural history." As you saw in each of the studies undertaken at Hubbard Brook, counting and getting numbers of each kind of organism was an important part of the work. To quantify something is to count it or show how much of it is present.

But ecology is much more than counting, and the ecologist is more than a counter. He or she recognizes the relationships—how one thing acts on another—in the total environment or ecosystem. Until relationships are known in any ecosystem, successful control and management of the resources on Planet Earth are difficult. We see the results of mismanagement daily in the newspaper headlines: flood, drought, endangered species, overpopulation, famine, energy crisis, mercury poisoning, oil spills. Some of the causes of inflation and unemployment can be traced to ignorant manipulation of our natural resources.

All parts of the environment are woven in an intricate web. When something happens to one strand of the web, it takes a lot of knowledge to know what may happen to all the other strands. As ecologists piece more ecosystem patterns together and design experiments that test each individual strand, managers of land and water will be able to predict more accurately what will happen when a forest is cut, a dam is built, or a field is sprayed with an insecticide.

GLOSSARY

Anaerobic decay The breakdown of energy-containing substances by the activity of bacteria and other microorganisms in the absence of oxygen.

Bacteria Very tiny, single-celled organisms that make their living by chemically altering materials around them. They can then absorb the changed materials into their own life-supporting system. *See* Nitrogen-fixing bacteria.

Base line The first or original measurement to which other following measurements can be compared to determine the amount of change or lack of change in a situation or condition.

Biologist A scientist who specializes in the study of living things and their life functions and activities.

Biomass The amount of living material in an organism or all organisms living in a specific area, often stated in grams per square meter.

Biosphere The thin layer of the earth, including its atmosphere, where living things are found.

Bomb calorimeter An apparatus for burning small amounts of matter to determine how much energy, measured in calories, the matter contains.

Botanist A scientist who specializes in the study of plants.

Calories Small units of measure of heat energy. Other types of energy are often expressed in terms of calories.

Canopy The upper layer of tree leaves in a forest.

Carnivores Animals that eat other animals.

Carrion Dead-animal material.

Carrying capacity A specific number of plants or animals that can be kept alive and healthy by the resources in a given environment.

Chlorophyll The green material, a pigment, in plants which captures light energy from the sun and makes that energy available for the plant to use to support its life.

Clear-cut An area within a forest where all trees have been cut down.

Climax community All the living things that are best adapted to living together and in the physical conditions of a specific environment so that they will reproduce themselves and the community will persist unchanged for many generations.

Community All the living things of many different kinds that are living together, interacting with each other, in a specific area.

Competition An interaction between living things that occurs when there is not enough of something present in the environment to support all of them.

Composition The kinds and amounts of living things present at a specific place, as in the species composition of a pond.

Conservation Man's careful and wise use of the things in his environment that are needed to live a healthy, meaningful life.

Control In science, that part of a study that is not altered by the researcher and so is used as a basis for comparison with some other part of the study that has had some change made.

Cutover Land that has been clear-cut.

Data Statements of observations gathered in a careful study and recorded, using measurements wherever possible.

Decay The breakdown of the complex materials of once-living things to less complex materials, usually as a result of the life activities of bacteria, fungi, and other living things.

Decomposers Those living things which break down dead material of formerly living things into carbon dioxide, water, and other nutrients.

Density The number of living things, such as plants, in a specific-sized area.

Detritivores Animals that eat dead things and the fragments of partly decomposed things.

Detritus Dead material, usually a fragment or fragments of partly decomposed formerly living things, such as leaf mold.

Ecology The science that involves the study of the ways living things interact with each other and with the physical environment.

Ecosystem The total of all living things, all the features of their physical environment, and all the interactions between them. The size of an ecosystem may be very small or very large.

Element Any substance that cannot be separated into different substances by chemical processes.

Energetics The study of energy—where it is located, the amount present, and how it moves within the system.

Energy The capacity to do work. In an ecosystem energy study, the potential energy of biomass may be expressed as Calories per hectare (C/h).

Energy budget An analysis of the amount of energy entering, contained in, and passed on by living things in an ecosystem.

Energy flow The movement of energy along a food chain.

Entomologist A scientist specializing in the study of insects.

Environment Conditions that surround and/or influence an object or a living thing.

Eutrophication Process by which water becomes overrich in nutrients, as the result of pollutants which act like fertilizer, and supports an overabundant growth of plants.

Food chain The sequence of living things that energy will pass through before being lost from the system as heat.

Food web Intermeshing of several food chains.

Frass Dry pellets of undigested plant material that has passed through the digestive tract of an insect and dropped as waste.

Geologist A scientist who specializes in the study of the physical aspects of the Earth and its history, looking especially at rocks and minerals and the physical forces that act upon them.

Geometrid A moth of the family whose caterpillars are called inch worms.

Grubs Generally, insect larvae or, specifically, beetle larvae.

Habitat The elements of the surroundings of a living thing that are important to the way it lives.

Hardwood forest A landscape covered with broad-leaved trees such as oaks, birches, beeches, or maples.

Hectare An area equal to about 2½ acres or 10,000 square meters.

Herbivores Animals that usually eat plant material.

Herpetologist A scientist who specializes in the study of reptiles and amphibians.

Heterocampa A genus of moths which includes the saddled prominent, an important insect of the hardwood forests of New England.

Humus Material in and on the upper layer of soil which includes all the formerly living matter that is in various stages of decay.

Ichthyologist A scientist who specializes in the study of fish.

Identification key Descriptions grouped so as to enable a person to identify an unknown specimen.

Igneous Rocks that have formed by solidification from the molten state.

Inorganic Composed of matter that is not and has not been an important part of the chemistry of living things. *See* Organic.

Input Materials and energy that are added to a system.

Instar A growth stage of an insect, between molts.

Intrasystem cycling The endless movement of a substance *within* an ecosystem. Each living thing (organism) may pass a substance on to another organism or back to the physical environment by the processes of eating, being eaten, or decomposition. This movement is along a food chain.

Invading species A kind of living thing that specializes in moving into and colonizing an environment, usually when the system has been upset by some disturbance such as a fire, severe damage from the wind, or an ice storm.

Invertebrates Animals that have no backbone or spinal column.

Leaching Dissolving and carrying away substances from the soil or plants by water passing through the soil or over the surface of a plant.

Life history A description of all important characteristics and events in the life of any organism: life-span, number of young, habitat, enemies, etc.

Limiting factor The part of an organism's environment that keeps it from becoming more numerous.

Limnologist A scientist who specializes in the study of bodies of fresh water and the things living in them.

Litter Plant and animal parts (e.g., leaves, limbs, feathers, frass) that have fallen to the surface of the ground.

Mammalogist A scientist who specializes in the study of mammals.

Mammals Warm-blooded animals that have hair or fur and whose young drink milk from their mother's body.

Materials Those substances (chemical elements and compounds) that are found in a system. In an ecosystem study, nutrient materials are of special interest.

Metabolism The process of the continuous chemical reactions that occur in a living thing.

Microclimates The average weather conditions (e.g., temperature, humidity, amount of sunlight) that occur in the immediate environment of an object or a living thing.

Microenvironment The specific conditions and organisms that are found in the immediate vicinity of a living thing and that directly affect it.

Microhabitat The specific physical conditions that exist in the close vicinity of a living thing. Microhabitat conditions may differ from general environmental conditions.

Microorganism A tiny living thing not visible to the naked eye. *See* Organism.

Molecule The smallest particle of an element or compound that can exist in the free state and still retain the characteristics of the element or compound.

Natural history The scientific study of nature.

Nitrates Chemical compounds that contain oxygen and nitrogen bound together in the ratio of three oxygen atoms to one nitrogen atom (NO_3).

Nitrogen A chemical element which occurs naturally by itself as a gas (78% of the Earth's atmosphere), and which combines chemically with other elements to become part of nitrates, proteins, etc.

Nitrogen-fixing bacteria Microorganisms that combine nitrogen atoms with other atoms, or "fix" the nitrogen, making it available for other organisms to use.

Nutrient A substance that living things can use for their growth and repair.

Nutrient budget An analysis of the amount of nutrients entering, contained in, and passed on by living things in an ecosystem.

Nutrient cycling The way in which nutrients move around through the ecosystem as in a food chain. *See* Intrasystem cycling.

Omnivores Animals that have a varied diet, eating plants and animals and sometimes also detritus or carrion.

Organic Composed of complex chemical substances built on the basis of chains of carbon atoms, these substances being the essential materials of all living things.

Organism An individual living thing, such as a plant, animal, bacterium.

Ornithologist A scientist who specializes in the study of birds.

Output Materials and energy that leave a system.

Overpopulation The presence of more individuals of a particular kind of living thing than the resources of an environment can support.

Oxygen consumption The amount of oxygen taken in by a living thing to use in the chemical reactions that must occur to support life activities.

Paleobotanist A scientist who specializes in the study of plant life which was on Earth in prehistoric times, using present-day evidence.

Parameters Measurements of particular aspects of something being studied, such as the numbers of individuals in a population, the numbers in each age level, or the sex ratio.

Photosynthesis The chemical process by which living things, mostly green plants, absorb light energy and build it into organic substances to be stored or used for growth and repair.

Phytoplankton Microscopic green plants which are free-floating in water.

Pioneer A kind of living thing that is among the first to colonize an environment newly made available to it by changes in that environment.

Pollution Undesirable amounts of substances or energy added to an environment, usually by man's activity.

Predator An animal that overcomes other animals in order to eat them.

Prey An animal that may be overpowered and eaten by another animal.

Primary consumer An animal that eats plant material.

Primary production The energy that is captured chemically by photosynthetic organisms. Net primary production is the energy stored in chemical form beyond the energy needed by the living thing to stay alive.

Recycle To reclaim useful material from waste and reuse it.

Secondary consumer An animal that eats other animals.

Sinks A general science term meaning withdrawal of something from a system. In ecology the term is used by some researchers to describe the temporary removal of certain nutrients from the available nutrient supply.

Species Indicates a class of individuals of a limited kind, having the same distinguishing characteristics and usually interbreeding only with their own kind.

Standing crop All the organisms of a particular kind, or all the organisms taken together, that are present in a given area at a specific time.

Steady state A balanced condition, so that an input to the system equals the output from the system, resulting in no observable change in the system.

Strip-cut A forestry practice in which bands of trees are cut down, with alternating strips of trees left standing.

Succession Over a period of time an orderly and gradual change in the plant and animal communities living in a specific area.

System In ecology, any group of living things and the physical features around them that relate to each other with flows of material and energy in continuing reaction; a self-sustaining, self-regulating group of relationships. An open system is a system that gains and/or loses materials or energy. A closed system is a system that has no gains or losses of material or energy.

Taxonomist A scientist who specializes in classification, or determining to which type of living things a particular individual belongs.

Terrestrial Having to do with land as opposed to water (aquatic).

Territory An area in which an animal lives and which it will defend against others of its kind.

Tolerance Ability of a living thing to survive in the presence of a specific material or condition.

Transect A line through an area along which samples are taken in a study to determine some property or properties of that area.

Transpiration The loss of water from leaves by evaporation.

Watershed The land surface area that is drained by a given steam.

Weir A small dam designed to be used in measuring the amount of water flow in a stream.

Windfall Trees that have been blown over by strong windstorms.

Zoologist A scientist who specializes in the study of animals.

Zooplankton Tiny animal life floating freely in the water.

FIELD GUIDES AND FURTHER READING

Alexander, Taylor R., and Fichter, George S., *Ecology.* Golden Press, 1973.

Bates, Marston, *The Forest and the Sea.* Random House, Inc., 1960.

Borror, Donald, and White, Richard, *Field Guide to the Insects.* Houghton Mifflin Company, 1970.

Brockman, C. Frank, *Trees of North America.* Golden Press, 1968.

Conant, Roger, *A Field Guide to Reptiles and Amphibians of Eastern and Central North America.* Houghton Mifflin Company, 1975.

Darling, Lois and Louis, *A Place in the Sun: Ecology and the Living World.* William Morrow & Company, Inc., 1968.

Farb, Peter, and others, *Ecology.* Time-Life Books, 1970.

Hoover, Helen, *The Long-shadowed Forest.* The Thomas Y. Crowell Company, Apollo Edition, 1968.

Leopold, Aldo, *A Sand County Almanac: With Other Essays on Conservation from Round River.* A Sierra Club/Ballantine Book, 1966.

Lorenz, Konrad Z., *King Solomon's Ring.* The Thomas Y. Crowell Company, 1952.

McCormick, Jack, *The Life of the Forest.* McGraw-Hill Book Co., Inc. 1966.

Mitchell, Robert T., and Zim, Herbert S., *Butterflies and Moths.* Golden Press, 1964.

Morgan, Ann Haven, *Field Book of Ponds and Streams: An Introduction to the Life of Fresh Water.* G. P. Putnam's Sons, Inc., 1930.

Murie, Olaus, *A Field Guide to Animal Tracks.* Houghton Mifflin Company, 1954.

Odum, Eugene P., *Ecology.* 2d ed. Holt, Rinehart & Winston, Inc., 1975.

Palmer, E. Laurence, and Fowler, H. Seymour, *Fieldbook of Natural History.* McGraw-Hill Book Co., Inc., 1975.

Peterson, Roger Tory, *A Field Guide to the Birds.* Houghton Mifflin Company, 1947.

Petrides, George A., *A Field Guide to Trees and Shrubs.* Houghton Mifflin Company, 1958.

Pringle, Laurence P., *Ecology: Science of Survival.* The Macmillan Company, 1971.

———*Into the Woods: Exploring the Forest Ecosystem.* The Macmillan Company, 1973.

Reid, George K., *Pond Life.* Golden Press, 1967.

Robbins, Chandler S.; Bruun, Bertel; and Zim, Herbert S., *Birds of North America.* Golden Press, 1968.

Russell, Helen Ross, *Earth, the Great Recycler.* Thomas Nelson & Sons, 1973.

Selsam, Millicent E., *Birth of a Forest.* Harper & Row, Publishers, Inc., 1964.

Shuttleworth, Floyd S., and Zim, Herbert S., *Non-Flowering Plants.* Golden Press, 1967.

Sparks, John, *Bird Behavior.* London: Hamlyn Pub. Group, Ltd., 1969.

Storer, John H., *The Web of Life.* The New American Library of World Literature, Inc., 1968.

Teale, Edwin Way, *The Strange Lives of Familiar Insects.* Dodd, Mead & Company, Inc., Apollo Edition, 1968.

Welty, Susan, *Birds with Bracelets: The Story of Bird-Banding.* Prentice-Hall, Inc., 1965.

Zim, Herbert S., and Hoffmeister, Donald, *Mammals.* Golden Press, 1955.

Zim, Herbert S., and Shoemaker, Hurst H., *Fishes.* Golden Press, 1956.

Zim, Herbert S., and Smith, Hobart H., *Reptiles and Amphibians.* Golden Press, 1953.

INDEX